THE LION
ROARS
Your Enemy Will Bow

Dr. Ron Kussmaul

KUDU

The Lion Roars: Your Enemy Will Bow

by Dr. Ron Kussmaul

Copyright © 2012 by Dr. Ron Kussmaul

Published by Kudu Publishing

Trade Paperback ISBN: 978-1-9386240-7-0
eBook ISBN: 978-1-9386240-8-7

Available in Amazon Kindle, Apple iBooks and Barnes & Noble Nook formats.

Cover Design: Martijn van Tilborgh

CONTENTS

INTRODUCTION

Many people fall prey to the wiles of the devil. I witness this situation in Christians from all occupations. When I go to cities and churches around the world, I find individuals who are victimized continually. They are always in a trap.

An old cliché says, "You can't see the forest for the trees." These Christian victims of life stand out in a crowd. I address this widespread problem from the perspective of a predator hunting for easy prey. The unseen spiritual predators who prey upon the souls of unsuspecting people do not overlook born again believers.

These unseen spiritual predators show no mercy and give no quarter in their vicious attacks. Their only motivation is *easy prey*. Both earthly and spiritual predators are similar in their tactics, seeking the *weak, crippled* and *stupid* among both the natural herd and the spiritual flock (church).

The Roar of a Lion will expose the tactics of the unseen predators. I believe it will give the body of Christ a fresh look into the deceptive methods of the demonic forces that lurk in the shadows of the spirit. It will define clearly how they look for flaws and weaknesses in a Christian's life.

In these pages, the devil's weakness is exposed and power in the mighty name of Jesus Christ is exalted.

Chapter 1

THE MIGHTY KING

In the tall grass of the veld, he will lie in wait.
There is no thought of any malice or hate.
Yes, in the tall grass is where he will wait,
But with one little mistake, it will be too late.
— Rev. Ron Kussmaul, Johannesburg, South Africa

The fiery orange orb of the sun sinks steadily in the western sky. The intensity of its heat burns through the dusty air. The gusty wind lifts little dust devils before his eyes as he gazes intently upon the panorama of life that lies before him. In another hour, the sun will be gone from his kingdom. As twilight creeps in, it changes the furnace effect of Africa's hot, dry air into the cool, slight dampness of night.

He has no understanding of the scientific reason for the temperature change that brings life-giving moisture to the ground. These things never seem important to him in the great scheme of life, for this is his kingdom and he is king of all he surveys. Not one of his subjects dare challenge him. He is the king of beasts, all 460 pounds of him, from the shining tip of his sensitive nose, down the length of his great black mane that hangs to the ground, to the tuft of black hair that covers the tip of his tail. He spent the heat of the day in the deep cover of the impenetrable jess, thick with thorns. He slept fitfully due to the hunger that rumbles through the deep recesses of his stomach. He enjoys the rich blood-laden flesh of Africa, as herds of his subjects delight his taste buds and bulge his sides, only to pass through his bowels to rejoin the food chain.

He settles into a comfortable position, with his massive head resting upon the dusty ground, and watches the small waterhole beside the dry buffalo grass. He dozes from time to time as he waits for his subjects to assemble before he makes his selection. His large nostrils rest upon the ground between his powerful paws. Every breath creates a tiny disturbance in the dust. As he slips in and out of sleep, he dreams of game, such as the zebra, with its huge shanks of flesh. He remembers the massive Cape Buffalo upon which he fed for days, while he kept the scavengers away from what belonged to him. That didn't matter now. He'd make another selection when his subjects came to pay homage.

Alert Now! Eyes blazing to the point that they seem to glow, they follow the stately kudu bull that, in a very skittish manner, slowly picks his way down to the far side of the waterhole. The distance is too far, but he'll build a false confidence in the others.

"They'll be moved by what they see, thinking I'm not here just because they can't see me. Some of my subjects are so stupid. This is the only waterhole for 20 square miles. Where else would I be?"

The great head sinks slowly to the earth again, as the yellow eyes close in slumber, dreaming of the sun-ripened carcass of an elephant. He and his pride of lionesses ate their way into that cavernous stomach cavity. Oh, the memories of past delights in his kingdom, not to mention his large harem and the wonder of the mating season where he lost as much as 50 pounds of his beautiful flesh while fulfilling his strenuous duty. Many generations have passed through his powerful loins to fulfill their destiny across the panorama of his vast domain.

Snort! Instantly alert to what spooked the kudu bull, as it finished quenching its thirst, he lay waiting like a coiled spring. He can hear the little hooves of the group of female impala long before they come into view. Too much trouble again, and too far away, so he eases back down from his position of alertness where he is ready to burst into full charge.

"Huh! In my younger days, I would have launched myself like a tawny yellow missile at the subjects on the other side of the waterhole. However, I've grown much wiser! I've learned the secrets of waiting. I think it's called patience. Yes, patience really is a virtue. All good subjects come to those who have the strength of waiting. If I wait a little longer one of the stupid subjects will come to me for selection." Our lion king doesn't know, nor can he understand, that patience is, indeed, a virtue. One of the definitions of virtue is effective power or force!

"Here I am dozing off to sleep again, dreaming of all the great kills and past feasts. Tonight I'd settle for a tough old warthog."

Our lion king never has heard of the award-winning movie, *The Lion King*. How is he to know that lions and warthogs are supposed to be good friends, have long chats and develop lifelong relationships? Now he's about to invite one for dinner–once! There's no mercy here. Our lion is out to kill, devour and destroy. He won't have a disturbed conscience nor feel any guilt or remorse.

The waterhole teems with life as the young frolic and the mature drink the precious life-sustaining liquid. There are many subjects within range of the hungry king, but he remains hidden and motionless in the tall grass. He has something special on his mind, and when he sees the subject with the right qualifications, he will spring into action.

There it is. The sound he's waited to hear–the sound of an arthritic, heavy beast moving slowly to water. Noisy, slow and clumsy, the big black subject parts the heavy grass and gazes with

9

longing at the warm brown water. The locals call the old Cape Buffalo a "dugga boy" because of the long hours he spends lying in the water and mud to soothe his almost useless, swollen joints. Now he lowers himself awkwardly into the muddy edge of the waterhole. Our lion king patiently waits for the old joints to become set into position. This will make his charge that much more successful. The old bull will have great difficulty gaining his feet, much less shuffling away to escape the king of the beasts.

Why did our lion choose this particular old bull for his feast? The bull once had shiny black horns 45 inches wide, able to hook and toss lions into a crippled mass. Time has splintered and worn these horns, making them useless for defense. He once ran with the herds and made the annual migration, but now he's a cripple, defenseless and unable to escape. Our lion king patiently waits for the right subject. If you are patient, the sick, feeble, weak, crippled and stupid will come.

Why is the lion king doing his own killing? I thought the lionesses always did that, and he just showed up for the meal, had his fill and gave them whatever remained. That is true when it comes to the king of the beasts, if he is still king! Unfortunately, just as in other places in this world, when the king of the beasts is past his prime, he is deposed, and a stronger one takes his place. This is the case of our subject lion. Our lion king dozes and dreams of past glories of the prime of life. Now, reality is about to be set in motion in a life-and-death struggle.

The old bull wallows and turns his back, while the lion musters all his strength for a ferocious charge. As he springs, he feels pain in his left shoulder where the bullet remains from the fire stick of the two-legged man-thing. All he did was kill and eat the small man-thing he found walking along the dirt road at night. That was long ago, yet he remembers how they hounded him. His great mane, now thin and scraggly, brushes the grass as he emerges from hiding. His ferocious roar bursts forth, far less spectacular than it once was. His lungs no longer carry the volume of air necessary to produce the earth shaking roars that keep his subjects suitably awed. It's necessary for him to keep them in fear of him, for if they discover the truth of his condition and natural ability to steal, kill and destroy, he'll lose what little control he still has over them. He must be able to maintain this great deception, or he himself will be lost.

He lands squarely upon the old buffalo's shoulder and takes one great swipe with his forepaw against the neck. Stunned, the buffalo falls back to the ground in a great cloud of dust, a few yards from where he was resting in the muddy waterhole. He quickly fastens himself to the old bull's throat and partly crushing, partly strangling, keeps the old beast on the ground, cutting off the air supply to the tired old lungs. After a full ten minutes, the great struggle ends. Life in the animal kingdom is cheap. There is no remorse for the necessary killing.

Panting from the strenuous fight that sapped his strength, our lion begins to partake of the sustenance that will revive him. Straining with the task, he hungrily tears at the carcass, for he knows he has little time to get his fill before the scavengers arrive. He no longer has the ability to keep them off his kill. The hyenas, jackals and vultures often gaze at him with a knowing demonic look. It won't be long before he will be merely a feast and not the king of beasts.

With a partially filled belly and fear of his future, he slowly slinks away into the cover of the darkness of night. He hears the sounds of the pack of hyenas, like demons, snapping and tearing at his kill. No longer is he a noble king, feared by his subjects. He that sowed so much fear and dread is now the recipient of what he has sown. The reality of his ultimate harvest is upon him and the truth is unavoidable.

What can we learn from this mighty lion king?

1. The strength and vitality of his reign is over.
2. He will only grow weaker.

Why do his subjects still fear him?

1. He smells, looks and acts like a lion.

2. They remember the ravenous beast of yesterday.

What are his weapons?

Deception and Fear

What do his subjects not know?

His power is broken.

Chapter 2

SELECTING VICTIMS

'Tis a season of training for ruling and reigning.
From dawn until dark, the lessons are straining.
But great strength and skill the little ones are gaining,
The result is that now the victim's blood they are draining.
— Rev. Ron Kussmaul, Johannesburg, South Africa

In Africa, this panorama of life and death continues, with the rewards going to the survival of the fittest. The strong survive and the weak are attacked. Nothing can change this as life continues from day to day.

Yes! This is a unique manner in which to unfold this book, but it lends itself well to the situation of ministry, life and travel in southern Africa.

From the moment they're born into this world, lions are king. They roam the African veld (pronounced "felt") to prey upon the flesh of those around them. The great herds migrate to follow the rains and grass. The great beasts of prey follow their migrations, the lion at the head of the list. Of all the creatures of the field, the lion represents a perfectly designed killing and devouring machine, with the natural instincts to complete the job quickly and efficiently.

An old adage says, "Practice makes perfect." This is true of many things. Indeed, a constant repetition of doing anything from the simplest to the most complicated task brings efficiency. The great cats instinctively develop a critical eye, as they go about their daily task of watching the herds move across the veld. Their eyes automatically recognize the weak–those who are young, weak or aged who cannot escape.

Another group upon which they prey are the cripples. They're easy to spot as they limp through life with a broken leg or a blind eye, damaged by fighting with each other.

The last group is one you wouldn't expect in the animal kingdom, those who are just plain stupid. They walk around as if in a daze, completely oblivious to the rest of creation around them. They live their lives by the law of averages.

No matter into which of the three categories they fall, they still are, technically, a cripple, and therefore easy prey for those who watch and wait, cloaked with the disguise of cunning, camouflage and deception. In this chapter, we'll focus upon the training and development of our lion's natural skills of selecting and killing.

From the moment he drew his first breath, as the lioness cleaned him and his sister, he felt safe and secure. He snuggled up next to that great warm, tawny body that represented both his food and security. He knew nothing of the world around him or the dangers associated with his coming kingdom. Instruction in the ways of life began as soon as his keen eyes opened. He learned the hard way that he had to obey his mother. Their first lesson was to remain in the thick grass and thorns where his mother hid them while she was off hunting. For his disobedience, he received more than one wallop to the head that sent him sprawling, head over heels. His training was hard. Disobedience brought strict discipline at a young age, because life is harsh, cruel and unforgiving.

An old male leopard took his sister when she went wandering down by the river while the lioness was off hunting. Death was instant. The young cub never knew what hit her. She made a slight "yip" as the powerful jaws of the leopard carried her into the tree. Life is hard and unforgiving and, as the old saying goes, "It's a jungle out there." Have you noticed it's no different in your own jungle?

His body filled out and the clumsiness of a young cub disappeared. Soon he began to accompany the lioness on the hunt. His first selection was a warthog piglet, which he easily caught. He didn't know he had to kill it. The lioness previously had killed all the prey that he'd seen. Each time he took his paws away, the piglet ran with a great burst of speed, making a game until he tired of it. With one quick bite to the neck, the game was over and the feast was on.

Oh, how sweet was that first innocent kill, but from that time he knew the power and strength that resided within him. The ability to kill swiftly with no remorse came automatically, born within and honed to a fine cutting edge. By daily practice and repetition, he became skilled in the tools of his trade.

An innate ability to spot the weak, crippled and stupid came easily as the lioness schooled him in the art of killing. There were many lessons to learn, but these three stood out in his training.

1. The development of a keen eye to select the right subject who is weak, crippled or stupid.

2. Stealth and deception to give the subject selected a false sense of security and safety.

3. Total commitment to a full charge, with no mercy given; one must kill the victim.

Having learned his lessons well, especially the ability to select the correct victim, he couldn't quite understand why the healthy and strong of the herds were terrified, but it made him feel good. Sometimes he'd strut down to the waterhole as if he owned the world and gloat as he watched his subjects tremble in fear, tuck tail and run. The lion king carefully developed his innate ability to steal, kill and destroy. He knew he had it and so did his subjects. They were in a life-and-death struggle on the dusty plains of the African continent. Selection is a never-ending cycle.

There remains only the playing out of the individual roles in this panorama of life that begins with the first intake of oxygen and ends as the last thoughts of consciousness recede into darkness. The role of predator and prey, the hunter and the hunted, continue in a daily struggle for existence. The cycle of life completes itself in the jungle once again.

What comprises the young lion's training?

1. Selection

2. Deception

3. Destruction, killing, giving no quarter and having no mercy

4. Repetition

Chapter 3

VICTIM CHARACTERISTICS

Look on the masses as they calmly pass by.
It's almost as if with a loud shout they do cry.
They do not blend in, but conspicuously stand out.
They seem to be saying, "I volunteer," with a loud shout.
— Rev. Ron Kussmaul, Johannesburg, South Africa

Our lion is capable of taking the young and vigorous almost as easily as the weak, crippled and stupid. The weakest automatically draw his attention because they are the easiest to kill. Like a moth to the light and a magnet to metal, the destroyer draws the weak, crippled and stupid ones who fear him greatly. The tactics of lying in wait and ambushing the victim with a swift, overwhelming charge is the method most often chosen by this great predator.

The *weak* fall easily to the lion, as they're unable to escape by their own strength. They live day to day by the law of averages.

They're saved by the vast size of the herd. When the lion selects others that fall prey, they escape to live another day. From the time of their birth until maturity, the weak fall easily to the great predators. The oldest in the herd experience the same susceptibility as they can't move quickly enough to escape or their eyesight begins to fail them.

The *cripples* are physically impaired in many different ways and, therefore, can't escape, once selected by the predators. The crippling effect may have occurred as a birth defect, or damage from an accident or some other occurrence of nature. They're hampered physically and unable to complete a successful escape.

I classify the last group as *stupid*. They seem to stumble through life, defying the law of averages, not using the abilities with which they were born: keen sight, smell and hearing to detect the approach of a predator. They usually are at the wrong place at the right time with a silly look on their faces and wonder, "Where did all the lions come from?" Sometimes this stupidity affords them a way of escape, as the predators stand and stare in total disbelief, unable to take advantage of their good fortune as the prey bounds off to live another day.

The great predators gravitate to the weak, crippled and stupid for an easy kill, as if drawn by a magnet. This group stands out like a sore thumb, as if they had a sign hanging around their necks reading, "Eat me!" This group is easy to kill, steal or destroy from among the great herds.

Every species on earth–from humans to dung beetles–has its vulnerable individuals. Born again believers in the body of Christ are no exception. This taking of the weak, crippled and stupid is actually nature's way of keeping a species free of birth defects, allowing the healthy to utilize the resources available, and, thus, sustain healthy herds.

You might say, "It sounds like the survival of the fittest." That's exactly what it is in this dog-eat-dog world. The strong survive to pass on their life and vitality, while the weak are devoured. Do the predators kill some of the strong and healthy animals? Yes, of course. The lion prefers the weak, crippled and stupid because they live by the law of averages. They make an easy target!

Chapter 4

NECESSARY CULLING

To destroy so you can save is a job for the strong and brave.
Life's course is hard and sometimes the weak must go to their grave.
Though by this action the strong from extinction we save,
This hard job requires a great heart, strong and brave.
— Rev. Ron Kussmaul, Johannesburg, South Africa

I trust you enjoyed our journey through the bush veld of Africa and your contact with the predators and prey. However, it's not only in the primitive areas of Africa and in the animal kingdom that the predators stalk their prey. They stalk in every country, in the cities, on the streets and in the suburbs looking for the weak, crippled and stupid to consume.

Let's understand the word cull. The word *cull* means *to pick out or select; to examine carefully in order to make a selection;* it also means *something picked out, especially something rejected as not up to standard.*

I want you to hold the last meaning in your mind. The substandard attract predators as a moth to a light. Likewise, the magnet automatically attracts metal with great force. The great predators, with that same unction, find the easy prey and select them from among others, determining that they are not up to standard and, therefore, an easy kill.

In the jungles of the large cities, this contact between predator and prey is played out every hour of the day. Human predators search out human victims that are not up to standard. They choose weak, crippled and stupid that live by the law of averages and are unable to fight and resist. They're as skilled at their trade as the African lion.

Necessary Culling is the title of this chapter. Whether or not you are aware of it, it takes place for a number of reasons. How could this be? What circumstances possibly could cause a situation that requires necessary culling?

In the United States, the whitetail deer population is at an all-time high. There are so many deer within the fenced areas of Chicago's O'Hare Airport that the deer are culled in order to curtail incidents on the active runways. In one year there were 47,000 highway accidents involving whitetail deer in Pennsylvania alone.

In southern Africa, I have lived through several periods of devastating drought. The livestock and wild animals feel the drought. The hardship extends also to the people as they suffer through daily life with little or no water. In the good years, the rains come on time, and the cycle of new growth on the plants and trees is enough to increase the herds of animals in a constant growth pattern.

The elephant is constantly on the move from place to place and can cover as much as 25 miles, foraging food and going to water. He eats up to 21 hours a day, consuming huge quantities of grass, tree bark, tree branches up to two inches thick and all varieties of palm, palmetto and water plants. To be in the presence of elephants and other game species is both pleasurable and very dangerous. During the good times, the herds increase until their numbers grow beyond the capacity of the land to sustain them. The elephant devastates its habitat even in the good years with normal rainfall, not to mention times of drought that last up to three or four years. During the good years, elephants congregate as long as the food supply remains.

This reminds me of the way some Christians congregate in church and feed upon the Word of God. They fill up, but never use the strength provided by the Word to do anything other than look for more food to satisfy their insatiable appetite. This is the ultimate downfall of the great pachyderm and the downfall of the Christian, as well.

But be ye doers of the word, and not hearers only, deceiving your own selves. James 1:22

As a Christian becomes self-deceived in hearing and never doing, so also the elephant eats and destroys the vegetation during the good rainy seasons. They're also self-deceived. The land fights back to produce more to sustain the herds until a demon called drought stalks the terrain. The rivers become sand and the lakes dwindle to small muddy depressions, unable to sustain the herds. The great animals slow their pace and the skin hangs in loose folds on their bodies as the grim reaper stalks the landscape.

The antelope fall in the thousands when the grass disappears. The elephant will follow. Decisions are made for the wildlife and domestic livestock in addition to humans. Meat is a needed protein and a decision is required. Do we let the herds die and leave tons of meat to rot in the sun or do we cull to sustain that which remains and feed the hungry population?

Necessary culling reduces the population of pachyderms to a level the land can sustain. This necessary culling is for the common good of the remaining elephants so that they don't eat themselves out of house and home.

(In westernized nations, we never face this grim situation. We have no reason to think about this life and death drama. I want you to think about it now in connection with your life in Christ Jesus as you walk in this world. Come to a good level of understanding of its importance to you and your family.)

It's hard to decide to cull the great herds. But the consequence of not doing so will bring the total destruction of the habitat that sustains the elephants. Habitat destruction will cause the elimination of a species. A natural drought is the lack of rain. It's totally beyond the elephants' control. They fall victim to it, eating all the food nature has provided.

A spiritual drought is the lack of spiritual rain that comes from heaven. This drought is self-created. The elephants' habitat is the forest, bush or river valleys of Africa. The Christians' habitat is the ever-living Word of God. When the elephants destroy their habitat, they run the risk of being culled. Due to outside circumstances, they fall into the category of weak, crippled and stupid. They're selected and removed.

When the Christian habitat (the Word of God) becomes denuded, dried up, compromised or ineffectively preached, then Christians slip into the category of weak, crippled and stupid. They become vulnerable to selection and removal as they fall below the acceptable standard caused by this spiritual drought and lack of nourishment.

Then was Jesus led up of the Spirit into the wilderness to be tempted of the devil. And when he had fasted forty days and forty nights, he was afterward an hungered. And when the tempter came to him, he said, If thou be the Son of God, command that these stones be made bread. But he answered and said, It is written, Man shall not live by bread alone, but by every word that proceedeth out of the mouth of God. Matthew 4:1-4

It makes one wonder about the statement, "You are what you eat!" Jesus made it plain that natural food alone never will sustain man. He must live by every Word that proceeds out of the mouth of God. Yes, in the animal kingdom it's necessary to protect the habitat by selected removal from the species. In this natural world, overpopulation and drought are unforeseen circumstances imposed upon the elephants by outside conditions beyond their control.

We're not dealing with elephants, however, but people. There's no lack of spiritual rain from heaven. The spiritual droughts we face come from outside circumstances or are self-induced. Whichever the cause, we suffer and become weak, crippled and stupid, ready to fall into the clutches of that spiritual predator of the souls of mankind, with no strength to escape.

The focus of this book is not the culling of elephants or other animals. Our focus is the useless slaughter of God's sheep because they are weak, crippled or (let's face it) stupid.

The prophet Hosea warned the Lord's people when he prophesied to them in Hosea 4, verse 1.

Hear the word of the LORD, ye children of Israel: for the LORD hath a controversy with the inhabitants of the land, because there is no truth, nor mercy, nor knowledge of God in the land.

The land was totally devoid of the truth, mercy and knowledge of the Lord. There was a condition of spiritual destruction or drought throughout the land. There was no spiritual food upon which the people could feed to become strong. This resulted in a condition of spiritual weakness and they became the prey.

My people are destroyed for lack of knowledge: because thou hast rejected knowledge, I will also reject thee, that thou shalt be no priest to me: seeing thou hast forgotten the law of thy God, I will also forget thy children. Hosea 4:6

Lack of knowledge destroyed the people–because they rejected it. They purposely turned their backs on the knowledge, truth and mercy of God. This decision was self-inflicted and created destruction. Notice the Lord speaks against the priests, or ministers, and declares they no longer will be priests to Him because they have forgotten His Laws.

Lack of knowledge destroyed one generation, but look at the collateral damage as a second generation encountered destruction because their parents forgot the law of God. The Word states, "...*seeing thou hast forgotten the law of thy God, I will also forget thy children.*"

When one generation backslides from the law, they influence the lives of their children who are raised without God's presence in the home.

Be not deceived; God is not mocked: for whatsoever a man soweth, that shall he also reap. For he that soweth to his flesh shall of the flesh reap corruption; but he that soweth to the Spirit shall of the Spirit reap life everlasting. Galatians 6:7-8

This generation rejected God's knowledge, and they and their children reaped a sad harvest as the Lord rejected them. People suffer and grow weak beyond the ability to support natural or spiritual life when destruction comes to their physical or spiritual habitat. In this weakened condition, they wander aimlessly, undernourished, existing day to day by the law of averages, until they fall prey to the predators.

What is the Christian habitat?
The Word of God and His Kingdom

Is it large enough to accommodate the masses of humanity?
There is always room for more.

What can the Christian use for food?
He can rely on the living Word of God.

Does God withhold nourishment from His people?
God never withholds. You may eat freely from His Word.

Why are some Christians in such weakened condition?
They've decided to linger in a spiritually drought-stricken church.

Chapter 5

CULLING OF GOD'S PEOPLE

In Old Testament times, the people lived by the law.
Justice always came swiftly when their lives had a flaw.
Yes, many times God would place a great hook in their jaw.
There was neither grace nor mercy living under the law.
— Rev. Ron Kussmaul, Johannesburg, South Africa

Has there ever been a time when it became necessary to cull God's people? What were the circumstances that led to the decision to implement such harsh action?

We find our answer throughout the Old Testament. God's people lived under the bondage of the disobedience brought upon them by Adam's sin. God placed His people under the protective covering of the law. He created rules and regulations of how to live. He created the blood sacrifice to atone for their sins.

We see that the major reason culling was necessary for the common good was because of the sin of disobedience to the law that God instituted to protect His people.

The Golden Calf

And when the people saw that Moses delayed to come down out of the mount, the people gathered themselves together unto Aaron, and said unto him, Up, make us gods, which shall go before us; for as for this Moses, the man that brought us up out of the land of Egypt, we wot not what is become of him. Exodus 32:1

The people were not to have other gods before Jehovah. After deliverance from the hand of Pharaoh, they transgressed His chief law. In Exodus 32, they demanded that Aaron, while Moses was still on the mount with God, make a golden calf.

And the LORD said unto Moses, Go, get thee down; for thy people, which thou broughtest out of the land of Egypt, have corrupted themselves: They have turned aside quickly out of the way which I commanded them: they have made them a molten calf; and have worshipped it; and have sacrificed thereunto, and said, These be thy gods, O Israel, which have brought thee up out of the land of Egypt. And the LORD said unto Moses, I have seen this people, and, behold, it is a stiff-necked people: Now therefore let me alone, that my wrath may wax hot against them, and that I may consume them: and I will make of thee a great nation. Exodus 32:7-10

The Lord told Moses the people had corrupted themselves by making a golden idol. Take special notice that *the people corrupted themselves* through disobedience by a wrong decision. This decision was a grievous sin with dire consequences for the whole nation. Watch as Moses separates the faithful.

Then Moses stood in the gate of the camp, and said, Who is on the LORD's side? Let him come unto me. And all the sons of Levi gathered themselves together unto him. Exodus 32:26

God sent the sword throughout the camp and destroyed the disobedient. Verse 28 says 3000 men died.

And the children of Levi did according to the word of Moses: and there fell of the people that day about three thousand men. Exodus 32:28

This is a clear example of the necessary culling for the greater good of the whole nation under the law. The Lord calls worshiping other gods or making idols to be self-corruption. The penalties are harsh. It was necessary to cleanse the spirit of disobedience from the congregation.

The Grasshoppers

But the men that went up with him said, We be not able to go up against the people; for they are stronger than we. And they brought up an evil report of the land which they had searched unto the children of Israel, saying, The land, through which we have gone to search it, is a land that eateth up the inhabitants thereof; and all the people that we saw in it are men of a great stature. And there we saw the giants, the sons of Anak, which come of the giants: and we were in our own sight as grasshoppers, and so we were in their sight. Numbers 13:31-33

The majority of the spies delivered an evil report to Moses about the Promised Land. This caused the people to murmur against Moses and Aaron. Because of the evil report, they become an evil congregation and refused to enter into the blessings the Lord had prepared for them.

How long shall I bear with this evil congregation, which murmur against me? I have heard the murmurings of the children of Israel, which they murmur against me. Say unto them, As truly as I live, saith the LORD, as ye have spoken in mine ears, so will I do to you: Your carcasses shall fall in this wilderness; and all that were numbered of you, according to your whole number, from twenty years old and upward, which have murmured against me, Doubtless ye shall not come into the land, concerning which I sware to make you dwell therein, save Caleb the son of Jephunneh, and Joshua the son of Nun. Numbers 14:27-30

The Lord called them an evil congregation and gave them what they spoke in His ears, even though it was not what they wanted. Only Joshua and Caleb lived to taste the goodness of the blessings in the Promised Land. Joshua and Caleb did no wrong. Their report was a good report. They knew the people were to go up at once to possess the land. However, they also paid a penalty created by the decision of the majority of the people. Though their faith-filled report kept them alive, they experienced the operating table of God for 40 years as His scalpel of time cut unbelief from among the people.

The disobedience of the majority postponed their destiny for 40 years. I'm sure Joshua and Caleb had no idea the other ten princes were going to give such a negative report. It made no difference. It cost them 40 years in the wilderness. Their destinies were put on hold.

There's a saying, "Birds of a feather flock together." It may benefit you to look at the "birds" with whom you flock. Decide if you want to associate with them and pay the same penalties they pay.

But your little ones; which ye said should be a prey, them will I bring in, and they shall know the land which ye have despised. But as for you, your carcasses, they shall fall in this wilderness. And your children shall wander in the wilderness forty years; and bear your whoredoms, until your carcasses be wasted in the wilderness. After the number of the days in which ye searched the land, even forty days, each day for a year, shall ye bear your iniquities, even forty years, and ye shall know my breach of promise. I the LORD have said, I will surely do it unto all this evil congregation, that are gathered together against me: in this wilderness they shall be consumed, and there they shall die. Numbers 14:31-35

Under the law of God, unbelief and disobedience had no place. For 40 years, the children of the disobedient generation wandered through the wilderness until the scalpel of time removed the last unbelieving person. This necessary culling was for the common good.

Korah's Rebellion

Keep focused on the fact that the word *cull* is *something picked out, especially something rejected as not up to standard.* The dispensation of the law did not tolerate unbelief and disobedience.

In Numbers, chapter 16, we see rebellion in the camp as Korah raised up 250 princes of the assembly against Moses. They took it upon themselves to minister before the Lord; yet didn't have the anointing to carry the office. This is basic rebellion and the Lord counts it the same as witchcraft and deals swiftly in His judgment of it.

Now Korah, the son of Izhar, the son of Kohath, the son of Levi, and Dathan and Abiram, the sons of Eliab, and On, the son of Peleth, sons of Reuben, took men: And they rose up before Moses, with certain of the children of Israel, two hundred and fifty princes of the assembly, famous in the congregation, men of renown: And they gathered themselves together against Moses and against Aaron, and said unto them, Ye take too much upon you, seeing all the congregation are holy, everyone of them, and the LORD is among them: wherefore then lift ye up yourselves above the congregation of the LORD? Numbers 16:1-3

In the ensuing confrontation between Moses and Korah's 250 rebels, we see necessary culling for the common good.

And the LORD spake unto Moses and unto Aaron, saying, Separate yourselves from among this congregation, that I may consume them in a moment. And they fell upon their faces, and said, God, the God of the spirits of all flesh, shall one man sin, and wilt thou be wroth with all the congregation? And the LORD spake unto Moses, saying, Speak unto the congregation, saying, Get you up from about the tabernacle of Korah, Dathan, and Abiram. And Moses rose up and went unto Dathan and Abiram; and the elders of Israel followed him. And he spake unto the congregation, saying, Depart, I pray you, from the tents of these wicked men, and touch nothing of theirs, lest ye be consumed in all their sins. Numbers 16:20-26

The ground swallowed Korah and his families, while fire came from the presence of the Lord and consumed the 250 princes who burned incense before the Lord.

And Moses said, Hereby ye shall know that the LORD hath sent me to do all these works; for I have not done them of mine own mind. If these men die the common death of all men, or if they be visited after the visitation of all men; then the LORD hath not sent me. But if the LORD make a new thing, and the earth open her mouth, and swallow them up, with all that appertain unto them, and they go down quick into the pit; then ye shall understand that these men have provoked the LORD. And it came to pass, as he had made an end of speaking all these words, that the ground clave asunder that was under them: And the earth opened her mouth, and swallowed them up, and their houses, and all the men that appertained unto Korah and all their goods. They, and all that appertained to them, went down alive into the pit, and the earth closed upon them: and they perished from among the congregation. And all Israel that were round about them fled at the cry of them: for they said; Lest the earth swallow us up also. And there came out a fire from the LORD; and consumed the two hundred and fifty men that offered incense. Numbers 16:28-35

The following day a plague came and destroyed 14,700 people because they accused Moses and Aaron of murdering the people. This was the direct result of blatant disobedience to the instructions and laws of God.

And the LORD spake unto Moses; saying; Get you up from among this congregation, that I may consume them as in a moment. And they fell upon their faces. And Moses said unto Aaron, Take a censer, and put fire therein from off the altar, and put on incense, and go quickly unto the congregation, and make an atonement for them: for there is wrath gone out from the LORD; the plague is begun. And Aaron took as Moses commanded, and ran into the midst of the congregation, and, behold, the plague was begun among the people: and he put on incense, and made an atonement for the people. And he stood between the dead and the living; and the plague was stayed. Now they that died in the plague were fourteen thousand and seven hundred, beside them that died about the matter of Korah. And Aaron returned unto Moses unto the door of the tabernacle of the congregation: and the plague was stayed. Numbers 16:44-50

God culled these rebels from the congregation for the good of the group at large (God's flock and the sheep of His pasture). God destroyed the rebellious when they disobeyed His laws. They were not up to God's standard. Their deaths saved the remnant of the people who did not corrupt themselves.

We must keep foremost in our minds that *we are talking about Old Covenant people* who didn't have the protection of the blood of the Lord Jesus Christ, with its access to God's grace and mercy. Their only protective covering was total obedience to the law and the atonement of their sins by the sacrifice of animals.

This was a dispensation where swift judgment and enforcement of the law overshadowed grace and mercy in order to protect the nation and secure the door of entrance for God's Son through the seed of David. An incorruptible seed couldn't arrive through the doorway of a corrupt nation.

Each time this necessary culling took place in the Old Testament, it was the direct result of rebellion or the disobedience of God's people, the king or the priesthood. We see plagues, pillage and bondage, but the common thread is blatant disobedience.

Yes, the Bible does show specific examples of the necessary culling of God's people for the ultimate protection and common good of the nation. The pure and simple reason was repeated disobedience.

Why was it necessary for God to take such harsh action?

The people corrupted themselves!

When you leave Christians without a vision for any length of time, they start to destroy themselves. Leave the Church alone and she will have strife, anger and bitterness. Eventually, for lack of anything better to do, she will split and go in separate ways, in spite of doing spiritual warfare against the devil.

The Church should not loiter in camp, but rather occupy this world in the name of Jesus.

Chapter 6

UNSEEN PREDATORS

Unseen spiritual predators are stalking this earth,
With most evil intent: death, famine and dearth.
They stalk through the land, they search and they seek,
Looking for Christians who are crippled and weak.
— Rev. Ron Kussmaul, Johannesburg, South Africa

In this world, the day-to-day struggle for survival continues as the natural predators weed out the weak, crippled and stupid. Predators cull them from the herds, rend the flesh and drink the blood, thereby providing energy for themselves and their offspring. They show no emotion and have no hatred toward their victims. This is "just another day at the office" for them as the panorama of life continues on the African veld.

How does this affect you and your family? You probably don't live in Africa. You're probably in a great city, suburb or rural area. You may live in a nation where wild animals are in a zoo or seen on Discovery Channel.

As the great predators roam the plains, valleys and bush of Africa seeking to destroy easy prey, so the great spiritual predators of our souls stalk the cities, suburbs and rural areas searching for easy prey. You guessed it. They're seeking the weak, crippled and stupid from among God's flock of sheep!

Are these unseen predators real? Yes, they're very real! Do they actually have the ability to prey upon us? Jesus bought us with His precious blood. The answer is "Yes." They can and do on a regular basis. I say this with one condition, so please hear me out.

These unseen spiritual predators are as large or small, as strong or weak, as you allow. The access and power they have over your life and family is limited to what you allow.

Your level of knowledge of them and of Jesus is the determining factor. From this point forward, we'll address this knowledge of the presence of Jesus within us as God-consciousness.

Finally, my brethren, be strong in the Lord, and in the power of his might. Put on the whole armour of God, that ye may be able to stand against the wiles of the devil. For we wrestle not against flesh and blood, but against principalities, against powers, against the rulers of the darkness of this world, against spiritual wickedness in high places. Ephesians 6:10-12

Yes, we're in a fight! It's the struggle between the sons and daughters of light and the forces of darkness. We're taught what to do, but rarely do we obey.

The Ephesians were instructed to be strong in the Lord and to use the power of His might, which means forcefulness. They were told to put on God's whole armor so they could stand against the wiles of the devil. These *wiles* are derived from the Greek word *methodeias*, meaning *the different means, plans and schemes used to deceive, entrap, enslave and ruin the souls of men.* The manner in which a person decides to sin is the devil's method of damning his or her soul. The Word of God further states that our fight is not against humans or this natural world. It's against unseen forces, principalities, powers, the rulers of darkness of this world and spiritual wickedness in high places.

Listed within *Vine's Dictionary*, in the category of beings called *daimonion*, are those that disseminate errors among men and those who seek to seduce believers. They're unclean in nature and can inflict bodily disease or cause one to fall into deception.

These unseen forces, principalities, powers, rulers of darkness of this world and spiritual wickedness in high places can use only the avenue of humanity that yields to them. It's not the people or circumstances against which we are wrestling, but the spirit of darkness behind them.

The instructions given to the Ephesians are easy to understand. This is the chapter where many people stray from the straight and narrow path and become obsessed with spiritual warfare and fighting the devil. Yes, I know we're in a fight, but we must remember what the prophet Hosea said.

My people are destroyed for lack of knowledge: because thou hast rejected knowledge, I will also reject thee, that thou shalt be no priest to me: seeing thou hast forgotten the law of thy God, I will also forget thy children. Hosea 4:6

The prophet didn't say they were destroyed for the lack of praying, but for the lack of knowledge. It's this lack of knowledge, or the ability to rightly divide the Word of God, that is one of the biggest hindrances to the believer today.

Study to shew thyself approved unto God, a workman that needeth not to be ashamed, rightly dividing the word of truth. 2 Timothy 2:15

One must *rightly* divide the Word of Truth in order to meet with God's approval. That means it's possible to wrongly divide the Word and be a shame unto God.

Will prayer change God the Father, Son or Holy Ghost? No, it will not. They're the same yesterday, today and forever (Hebrews 13:8).

Will prayer change our adversary, the devil? No, it won't. The devil has remained consistent and diligent for centuries and will remain so until he's cast into the lake of fire that burns forever. Consider his works. Lucifer aspired to be God, and that hasn't changed regardless of centuries of prayer. He deceived Eve in the garden, he deceived last year, last month, last week, today and he will lie and deceive tomorrow. The devil is consistent and will be until the end. The devil tries to take the place of Jesus, the same yesterday, today and forever. Consequently, the devil acts consistent in that he also is the same yesterday, today and forever, with one great exception. Jesus gives life and life more abundantly, while the devil steals, kills and destroys.

Am I against praying? Certainly not. *Prayer changes us!* Prayer changes people and people can change things. That is the whole key.

My wife and I were walking through the streets of Lisbon, Portugal, with our older son and his wife when we came to the corner of a wide boulevard. As I looked up the street, the traffic light changed and six lanes of traffic started down the road toward us. Based upon what I saw, I stayed on the sidewalk. My son, being his father's boy, jumped off the curb and ran across the street, pulling his wife behind him. Like a racehorse out of the chute, I followed as the traffic bore down on us.

Gaining the other side, I looked at him and said, "I wish I'd thought of that." Ron Jr. looked me in the eye and said, "Dad, life is just a bunch of decisions, some good, some bad and some that are ho-hum." At that moment the Holy Spirit spoke in my heart and said, "That's a great analysis of life, a number of decisions that are good, bad or ho-hum. Each decision carries its own blessing or penalty."

See, I have set before thee this day life and good, and death and evil; In that I command thee this day to love the LORD thy God, to walk in his ways, and to keep his commandments and his statutes and his judgments, that thou mayest live and multiply: and the

LORD thy God shall bless thee in the land whither thou goest to possess it. But if thine heart turn away, so that thou wilt not hear, but shalt be drawn away, and worship other gods, and serve them; I denounce unto you this day, that ye shall surely perish, and that ye shall not prolong your days upon the land, wither thou passest over Jordan to go to possess it. I call heaven and earth to record this day against you, that I have set before you life and death, blessing and cursing: therefore choose life, that both thou and thy seed may live: That thou mayest love the LORD thy God, and that thou mayest obey his voice, and that thou mayest cleave unto him: for he is thy life, and the length of thy days: that thou mayest dwell in the land which the LORD sware unto thy fathers, to Abraham, to Isaac, and to Jacob, to give them. Deuteronomy 30:15-20

Armed with the knowledge of who you are in Christ and who your adversary is, you will be able to identify and ward off every one of his methods of capture. How is this possible? Use Holy Ghost power to make the correct decisions for your life!

The greatest battle the Christian ever will fight is on the battleground of the mind. There is no battle against the devil in this natural world! Jesus fought and won that battle. He doesn't have to fight it again. The devil is a defeated foe, but he's still a foe. There's definitely a battle with sin, the flesh and the devil, but that comes back to making correct decisions for your life.

To reiterate, the only battle on earth between God and the devil is already over. It was a battle fought to redeem mankind and to gain access for us to return to the presence of God. Jesus Christ has obtained the victory! You don't have to try to fight that struggle again. To tell you the truth, you couldn't win, anyway.

Little children, let no man deceive you: he that doeth righteousness is righteous, even as he is righteous. He that committeth sin is of the devil; for the devil sinneth from the beginning. For this purpose the Son of God was manifested, that he might destroy the works of the devil. 1 John 3:7-8

Jesus won the battle of the ages when the Father sent Him to destroy the works of the devil. His battle was to defeat the enemy and give us victory over the devil. Jesus won that victory for us. It is finished! Jesus has fulfilled His Father's purpose.

Works is translated *work, employment and task.* Jesus Christ literally destroyed the devil's job. Think of it this way, the devil is *unemployed!* He's out of a job.

Our part of this divine connection is to enforce Satan's defeat through the power of choice. We *decide* not to commit sin and be drawn or enticed into the devil's traps to ensnare our souls.

I'm not a demon-chaser. I don't try to see a demon in every-thing or everyone. That's sheer nonsense. I'm not advocating that demons have power over God's children. Christians can and do make decisions to step outside the blood covering of Jesus and, thereby, *compromise their lives by opening a door of access.* It's through these incorrect decisions that demonic forces have ac-cess to wreak havoc in the lives of many in the flock of God.

Here's an example. A born again, Holy Spirit baptized believer teaching Sunday School can make a decision to yield to the lust of the flesh and look at pornographic material. This decision, once made, opens an area of one's life to the devil. The lust of the flesh is one of the devil's methods of seducing the souls of people. If not stopped and true repentance expressed, this Christian can become oppressed or completely possessed and controlled by the devil. Many in the Church fall in this area.

Behold, I give unto you power to tread on serpents and scorpi-ons, and over all the power of the enemy: and nothing shall by any means hurt you. Luke 10:19

Jesus spoke these Words to His disciples. The same strength and power is available to us today. The power in the name of Jesus is greater than *all* the power of the enemy. That would be enough, but He is the God of more than enough and completes the verse by saying, "and nothing shall by any means hurt you."

If this is true, why are so many in the Church weak, sick, hurt, confused and taken captive by the devil?

They *made a choice* to do things, go places or conduct their lives contrary to the Word of God and His divine will. Given these decisions, Christians place themselves outside the protection Jesus provided and begin to live a life that is not up to standard for a believer. They become weak to the lust of the flesh, crippled in their decision-making abilities to close this spiritual door and do stupid things. In this condition, they stand out in a crowd and become easy prey for the predator.

Do you remember the invisible spiritual predators? Let's look into the realm of the spirit. There are invisible beings watching you right now. You can't see them with your physical eyes, nor hear them with your physical ears, but they're there.

They can see in the spirit realm and the natural realm, so they see you and they hear you. This is a rather unique advantage for them, isn't it? Think about it right where you are at this moment!

In what jungle of the world do you live, walk, work, play and raise your family? Is it New York, Paris, London, Hong Kong, Johannesburg, the mountains, the coast, a small town or the desert? The unseen spiritual predators are there with you. They're watching and waiting to capture your soul.

I didn't create this picture to produce fear in your heart. I don't need to do that. Christians are full of self-created fears. They're afraid to pay their tithe, afraid to witness to the lost and afraid of the preacher. The preacher is afraid of the people and afraid other preachers in town will steal some of his people.

Another way of looking at the word fear is:

Fantasized Events Appearing Real

This fear grows even larger when we think on negative events, which we don't want to manifest in our lives. People say, "What's the worst thing that can happen in this situation?"

I created this picture into the spirit world to produce knowledge, to give you an advantage over these ruthless predators and to turn the fear in your heart into freedom and faith. These unseen spiritual predators steal, kill and destroy. They give no quarter, have no mercy and feel no remorse.

Chapter 7

CRIPPLED CHRISTIANS

Across this whole earth they do move and go,
But God's Word and God's ways they do not know.
They pray and they cry, yet remain ensnared, unable to break
The hold of the devil for lack of the Word's intake.
— Rev. Ron Kussmaul, Johannesburg, South Africa

What is a crippled Christian? Are there really such people? If so, how did they slip into this condition?

These definitions are from the *Webster's Ninth New Collegiate Dictionary*. The first definition of a *cripple* is *a lame or partly disabled person or animal; something flawed or imperfect.*

The word *crippled* (with an 'ed' ending) has a double meaning. *1. to deprive of the use of a limb and especially a leg. 2. to deprive of strength, efficiency, wholeness or capability for service.*

Please take notice that I don't say these things to be derogatory to any individual. My purpose is to show the correlation to the spiritual condition of many Christians.

We must ask these questions. How can a born-again person be flawed or imperfect? How is a Christian deprived of strength, efficiency, wholeness or capability for service when they have every right to use the power backed by the mighty name of Jesus? We are not speaking of the naturally crippled, but the spiritually crippled or impaired. For our answer, we must turn to the Word of God.

And these are they which are sown on good ground; such as hear the word, and receive it, and bring forth fruit, some thirtyfold, some sixty, and some an hundred. Mark 4:20

In explaining the parable of the sower to His disciples, Jesus spoke of the good ground being those who:

1. Hear the Word

2. Receive it

3. Bring forth fruit, some 30, some 60 and some 100

This doesn't show different *kinds* of Christians. This teaches different *degrees of fruitfulness* in the lives of Christians. When a Christian hears the Word of God, receives and is obedient to it, he or she will produce fruit.

If some produce 30, some 60 and some 100, this is a clear indication of different levels of hearing, receiving and obeying. These different levels not only affect the fruit a Christian produces but also indicate the levels of commitment and ability to make decisions. This level of fruitfulness will reflect in each life at the same degree in every area.

30-fold ability to shun the wrong and do the right

30-fold ability to love their neighbor

30-fold ability to tithe and give offerings

30-fold commitment to the local church

30-fold ability to be led by the Holy Spirit

30-fold ability to resist the devil

30-fold ability to forgive others

30-fold ability to receive and keep their healing

I minister around the globe and deal with pastors who tell me they spend most of their time counseling people. Many of these counseling sessions are with repeat customers.

What do we call Christians who hang in limbo, never grow spiritually and consistently do the wrong thing at the right time? They live a flawed or imperfect life and seem to have no strength to overcome their problems and make spiritually correct decisions. We'll place them in a category called "unbelieving believers." We could call them *crippled Christians*!

Let me clarify something. None of us has reached the area of perfection or maturity of our example, Jesus Christ. Don't read anything into the word *imperfect* in the preceding paragraph. I know that none of us is perfect. We still will be growing when we depart this world, but far too many are crippled Christians and are easy prey for the predators of darkness.

Crippled Christians (crippled sheep) live out their flawed, imperfect lives going to church while spiritually limping along and becoming a hindrance to the growth of the local congregation (local flock) to which they belong.

A Christian doesn't have a multiple choice of four or five different ways to live. The Bible is explicit.

Now the just shall live by faith: but if any man draw back, my soul shall have no pleasure in him. Hebrews 10:38

God didn't say to live by faith on Monday, Wednesday and Friday, and the rest of the week you'll be all right. He didn't say His soul has some pleasure in the person who lives that way. The Word of God is clear and understandable so that we can hear it, receive it and obey it.

If a person is only a 30-fold Christian, what's the remaining 70-fold? The forces that have access into this 70-fold uncommitted and wavering area include fear, compromise, confusion and disobedience.

There is therefore now no condemnation to them which are in Christ Jesus, who walk not after the flesh, but after the Spirit. Romans 8:1

The born again believers who walk after the Spirit will walk without condemnation, and those who walk after the flesh will have condemnation. There is no way to ascertain the percentage of believers who live under condemnation because they live according to the dictates of the flesh. In this condition, they fit the description of a crippled Christian. They live a flawed, imperfect Christian life, deprived of the strength, power and authority that Jesus gave.

1. The devil lies.

2. The flesh condemns.

3. The Holy Spirit convicts. Conviction has within it the ability, when acted upon, to release us from sin and change our ways, to be free from the condemnation of the flesh.

For they that are after the flesh do mind the things of the flesh; but they that are after the Spirit the things of the Spirit. For to be carnally minded is death; but to be spiritually minded is life and peace. Because the carnal mind is enmity against God: for it is not subject to the law of God, neither indeed can be. So then they that are in the flesh cannot please God. Romans 8:5-8

What a terrible condition this is, to be born again and walking 30-fold by the Spirit, and 70-fold by the dictates of the flesh. In this condition, they cannot please God, and they become easy prey for the unseen spiritual predators lurking nearby.

Imagine how difficult it is to get your prayers answered if you cannot please God!

For as many as are led by the Spirit of God, they are the sons of God. Romans 8:14

What are the characteristics of the sons of God?

The Spirit of God leads them and they produce the fruit of the Spirit in their lives.

But the fruit of the Spirit is love, joy, peace, longsuffering, gentleness, goodness, faith, meekness, temperance: against such there is no law. And they that are Christ's have crucified the flesh with the affections and lusts. If we want to live in the Spirit, let us also walk in the Spirit. Galatians 5:22-25

What are the characteristics of crippled Christians?

Their character reveals the scars of the works of the flesh.

Now the works of the flesh are manifest, which are these; Adultery, fornication, uncleanness, lasciviousness, Idolatry, witchcraft, hatred, variance, emulations, wrath, strife, seditions, heresies, Envyings, murders, drunkenness, revellings, and such like: of the which I tell you before, as I have also told you in time past, that they which do such things shall not inherit the kingdom of God. Galatians 5:19-21

They never will live the victorious life that Jesus purchased for them while they exist under fleshly condemnation. They remain crippled and vulnerable to spiritual predators.

In this condition, they're doomed to walk a flawed, imperfect life, deprived of strength, efficiency, wholeness or capability for service. We find them rejoicing on the mountaintops one moment and deep in the valley of the flesh the next. This up-and-down existence describes the lives of too many sons and daughters of God.

Listen to the testimonies of people. The disastrous details of what the devil has done will chill you to the bone. Their last sentence will be, "But, praise God, He gave me strength and brought me through."

The sinless sacrifice of Christ took place to give us life, and life more abundantly, not mere existence. Jesus made us alive unto God, free from existence under the merciless heel of the devil. You and I existed before Jesus came into our lives. He bore the burden of death, burial and resurrection so we could live abundantly!

Are you deprived of strength, efficiency, wholeness or the capability for service?

Jesus died on the cross of Calvary so you could do more than exist!

Chapter 8

YOUR ADVERSARY

Though broken and weak, his works do abound.
Yes, he lies and deceives using little strength or sound.
When there are gaps in the hedge of faith to be found,
Your life will fall prey to this merciless hellhound.
— Rev. Ron Kussmaul, Johannesburg, South Africa

Yes, we do have an adversary. He remains consistent in setting snares and destroying the souls of mankind. The *failure to identify* our adversary is the chief reason for his ability to destroy the sheep of God's flock. Insufficient and incorrect information about our adversary forms an incorrect image of who he is and what he can do.

My people are destroyed for lack of knowledge: because thou hast rejected knowledge, I will also reject thee, that thou shalt be no priest to me: seeing thou hast forgotten the law of thy God, I will also forget thy children. Hosea 4:6

Lack of knowledge will bring destruction. The adversary we face is none other than the devil himself. Do we need to pray harder to fight him? Prayer never hurts, but in this situation, the Word of God tells us we're lacking information.

Be sober, be vigilant; because your adversary the devil, as a roaring lion, walketh about, seeking whom he may devour: Whom resist stedfast in the faith, knowing that the same afflictions are accomplished in your brethren that are in the world. 1 Peter 5:8-9

The Bible clearly states the devil is our adversary. The word *adversary* is defined as *an opponent (in a lawsuit); the devil as the archenemy.* There are two sides in any lawsuit, the defendant, the one defending himself (sometimes called the accused) and the plaintiff, the one who brings the suit or accusation against the defendant.

And the great dragon was cast out, that old serpent, called the Devil, and Satan, which deceiveth the whole world: he was cast out into the earth, and his angels were cast out with him. And I heard a loud voice saying in heaven, Now is come salvation, and strength, and the kingdom of our God, and the power of his Christ: for the accuser of our brethren is cast down, which accused them before our God day and night. Revelation 12:9-10

The devil is the accuser in this court case where the defendant is the born-again believer. This accuser prosecutes his case 24 hours a day, searching for evidence to bring a verdict against the children of God. Unless there is clear evidence against the defendant, there is no case for the plaintiff to pursue, and there can be no judgment lodged. False accusations won't stand the test of the great courtroom of God's grace and mercy.

Ye are of your father the devil, and the lusts of your father ye will do. He was a murderer from the beginning, and abode not in the truth, because there is no truth in him. When he speaketh a lie, he speaketh of his own: for he is a liar, and the father of it. John 8:44

Your adversary is a liar. He lies and accuses you in an attempt to bring a charge against you in God's court to destroy your soul and pull you into hell. The good news is that you and I have an advocate to plead our case before the judgment bar of God.

My little children, these things write I unto you, that ye sin not. And if any man sin, we have an advocate with the Father, Jesus Christ the righteous: And he is the propitiation for our sins: and not for ours only but also for the sins of the whole world. And hereby we do know that we know him, if we keep his commandments. He that saith, I know him, and keepeth not his commandments, is a liar, and the truth is not in him. But whoso keepeth his word, in him verily is the love of God perfected: hereby know we that we are in him. 1 John 2:1-5

The Apostle John wrote about these things so that we wouldn't sin. If we do, the evidence on our lives is readily apparent to all.

For the wages of sin is death; but the gift of God is eternal life through Jesus Christ our Lord. Romans 6:23

John understood that the wages (paycheck) for sin is death. This is true in both the natural and the spiritual, where (in the spiritual) it means total separation from God, or spiritual death. He also knew Jesus Christ would be our advocate. He knew we could run to Jesus with a repentant heart and be released from our sins. He knew we could be cleansed by His sacrifice and not receive the paycheck for our sin, even though we earned it.

The invisible adversary is ruthless. He accuses the Christian day and night, but he must find evidence to build his case. If we run to our advocate Jesus Christ and repent of our sins, the evidence vanishes before he can complete his case against us.

We consider a thief or murderer to be a criminal. He or she remains unpunished if there isn't any incriminating evidence. Without evidence, there is no way to prosecute the case, display the burden of proof and pronounce judgment.

Our advocate faces a problem. How is He to defend the case of a crippled Christian when there is so much incriminating evidence lying around the scene of spiritual crimes (sins)? Our advocate is Jesus, The Way, The Truth and The Life. It's not possible for Him to lie when He pleads our case before the court of God. Jesus can present only the evidence that is visible in our lives. If the evidence substantiates their guilt, believers remain guilty as charged until repentance comes to the heart.

Behold, I give unto you power to tread on serpents and scorpions, and over all the power of the enemy: and nothing shall by any means hurt you. Luke 10:19

Jesus gave us power over three things: serpents, scorpions and all the power of the enemy. That is *all* the power of the enemy, not just some of it. If this is true, why are so many Christians bruised and beaten down by the devil when he has no legal rights?

Crippled Christians have too much self-incriminating evidence at the scene of the sins of daily life. Their adversary has enough evidence against them that he doesn't have to fabricate any. Their decisions and actions have condemned them to judgment, even though a way is available to be free and without sin through the sacrifice of Jesus. They surrender their position of power by willful disobedience and place that power in the hands of the devil.

The devil continually is looking for opportunities to gain power over the lives of God's people as they disobey the Bible. The devil, as a roaring lion, walks about seeking whom he may destroy. He cannot destroy just anyone he wants to destroy! He has to seek for people to destroy. He is *not* a roaring lion! The Word of God says, "*as* a roaring lion." He walks around <u>pretending</u> to be a lion that can devour.

When a real roaring lion stalks across his domain, he looks for easy prey upon which to fall and devour. When your adversary stalks this earth, he also looks for easy prey upon which to fall and devour. The word *devour* means *to gulp down and to swallow up*. In the same manner as the natural lion, our adversary must seek whom he may devour. He doesn't have the power to devour everyone he wants to destroy.

Take a good look behind yourself. What do you see?

Are you looking at evidence your adversary can use against you?

Is sin strewn across your path like yesterday's clothing on the bedroom floor?

If this is the case, your adversary is taking notes and you have tied Christ's hands. He cannot help you plead your case.

Chapter 9

ON THE PROWL

Those sitting in darkness, they prey upon the most.
Yet given the chance, they will destroy from God's host.
They kill and plunder unsuspecting lives, then boast.
To end this destruction Jesus came and gave up the ghost.
— Rev. Ron Kussmaul, Johannesburg, South Africa

A s the day dawns, the sons of men begin to shake themselves from slumber and rise from their beds to face the new day. The unseen adversary of the souls of men smiles as he contemplates his unsuspecting subjects.

"I am the prince of darkness and the prince of this world. The spirit of darkness covers those who belong to me. I have complete control over their lives, families and destinies. They are doomed to the slaughter and don't even know it.

"Another day to walk about and seek the ones I can destroy. They're so stupid. They don't think. They forget I'm around. Where else would I be? I enjoy lurking in the shadows and waiting for the right opportunity to strike fear in their hearts and swallow them. It never ceases to amaze me that they think I'm some sort of 'hob goblin.' They forget that I'm a real created being. I stand just beyond the veil of the flesh without a physical body, but I'm here and I'm well organized.

"I've organized one-third of the angels of heaven into ranks of principalities, powers, rulers of the darkness and spiritual wickedness. They assist me as I judge the people of this world and pronounce damnation upon their souls. Just as my eternal enemy, Jesus, knows His own, and they hear His voice, I know my own, and they obey me as long as they stay in darkness.

"I hate the light, any light, but especially the light of the gospel. It has the ability to shine into the hearts and minds of mankind and set them free from the darkness. I prefer them bound in chains and completely unaware!

"I hate the light anywhere I find it, but especially in the lives of Christians. They don't know how they appear in the spirit world. They shine brilliantly and cause us terrible problems because we can't stand that brightness."

Ye are the salt of the earth: but if the salt have lost his savour, wherewith shall it be salted? It is thenceforth good for nothing, but to be cast out and to be trodden under foot of men. Ye are the light of the world. A city that is set on an hill cannot be hid. Matthew 5:13,14

"I hate the words of Jesus, but I use them to form traps. Sometimes I use them to catch these sons and daughters of light. They don't realize how their lives glow when compared with those who sit in darkness. I'm sure they'd change and live differently if they knew I was watching for flaws in their garments."

Keep yourselves in the love of God, looking for the mercy of our Lord Jesus Christ unto eternal life. And of some have compassion, making a difference: And others save with fear, pulling them out of the fire; hating even the garment spotted by the flesh. Jude 21-23

"Yes, they may be the light of this world, but the words of Jesus have become a trap to many of the stupid ones. They can't hide from my careful scrutiny. They can't hide their weaknesses and sins from me. They can't know what I know about how easy it is to ensnare them. If they discover that they're wearing spotted and wrinkled garments they'll repent and change."

And unto the angel of the church in Sardis write; These things saith he that hath the seven Spirits of God, and the seven stars; I know thy works, that thou hast a name that thou livest, and art dead. Be watchful, and strengthen the things which remain, that are ready to die: for I have not found thy works perfect before God. Remember therefore how thou hast received and heard, and hold fast, and repent. If therefore thou shalt not watch, I will come on thee as a thief, and thou shalt not know what hour I will come upon thee. Thou hast a few names even in Sardis which have not defiled their garments; and they shall walk with me in white: for they are worthy. He that overcometh, the same shall be clothed in white raiment; and I will not blot out his name out of the book of life, but I will confess his name before my Father, and before his angels. He that hath an ear, let him hear what the Spirit saith unto the churches. Revelation 3:1-6

"I see them in their weakness as they limp through life. They're so deprived, inefficient, broken and good for nothing. It's obvious they're oblivious to the fact that I know these things."

Wherefore, my beloved brethren, let every man be swift to hear, slow to speak, slow to wrath: For the wrath of man worketh not the righteousness of God. Wherefore lay apart all filthiness and superfluity of naughtiness, and receive with meekness the engrafted word, which is able to save your souls. But be ye doers of the word, and not hearers only, deceiving your own selves. James 1:19-22

"These cripples stand out like neon signs in their self-deception and compromise. They're so easily snared. I'm willing to wait for the best opportunity to get them. They're always open to me!"

Nevertheless the foundation of God standeth sure, having this seal, The Lord knoweth them that are his. And, Let everyone that nameth the name of Christ depart from iniquity. 2 Timothy 2:19

"I have such fun tormenting these Christians who refuse to turn away from iniquity. They snap and snarl at each other for selfish reasons. They're mean and ugly to the ones who love them most. They find themselves at the wrong place at the right time and walk into my snare. Once taken, you should hear them scream and plead with God! Oh, they wail and cry, but it's too late."

Flee also youthful lusts: but follow righteousness, faith, charity, peace, with them that call on the Lord out of a pure heart. But foolish and unlearned questions avoid, knowing that they do gender strifes. And the servant of the Lord must not strive; but be gentle unto all men, apt to teach, patient, In meekness instructing those that oppose themselves; if God peradventure will give them repentance to the acknowledging of the truth; And that they may recover themselves out of the snare of the devil, who are taken captive by him at his will. 2 Timothy 2:22-26

"Christians actually *oppose themselves* when they are disobedient. They fall into harm's way where I snare them at my will. If I were a pastor, I'd have difficulty dealing with people who always oppose themselves and fall into snares. They require too much of a pastor's time and tons of patience. That would be okay if they grew, but most seem never to change their ways. They cry at the foot of the cross and plead the blood of Jesus as they limp through life. They live from one catastrophe to another, in spite of their great expenditure of time and prayer.

"Yes, I take them captive when I want, and they have no recourse. They remain captive because of their crippled condition. Many of them can't remember the promises or power of God. They just lie down and whimper as they accept their fate.

"Look at them, God. They're unable to defend themselves. They're powerless. Where's all that power You gave them? They are mine! I'm the prince of this world!"

Thou believest that there is one God, thou doest well: the devils also believe, and tremble. James 2:19

This is a great time to check your spiritual garment.

1. Are you satisfied with the condition it is in right now?

2. If the answer is no, are you willing to clean it up?

Suggestion: You'd take your clothes to the dry cleaners or put them in the washing machine. You'd feel no pressure or condemnation whatsoever. The precious blood of Jesus, when applied, will remove any spiritual stain.

Repentance is the only true stain remover!

Chapter 10

BIRTH DEFECTS

If while running this great race of life, I could find
A multitude of Christians who were not spiritually blind.
They could stop running in fear, and look around to find
That with the mighty name of Jesus the enemy they could bind.
— Rev. Ron Kussmaul,Johannesburg, South Africa

An animal with a birth defect stands out among the others in the herd; it's inferior due to the handicap. The game ranger will remove this animal from the herd so it can't reproduce that defective gene. When we remove this animal, we say it's culled. The animal is culled from the herd for the greater good of the whole. Tuskless elephants are culled from Africa's great herds for this reason. This wasn't done years ago and now the herds suffer. Let me explain.

There are tuskless bulls and cows in the herds due to the propagation of elephants with a weak gene. The bachelor herds kick out the tuskless bulls because they're weak and defective. The social order of the herd culls them, but in so doing, the problem actually is compounded.

These defective bulls remain with the cows and calves and perform their dominant role among the females. During the mating season, all the bulls are enticed by the heavy scent of the cows, but the tuskless bull is already there with them. Because he is the first on the scene, he mates with the herd cows before the healthy bachelor bulls can charge in. The defect is reproduced, weakening future generations.

You may wonder where I want to go with this train of thought, but bear with me. I'm not concerned with a defective physical gene. I'm concerned with a defective spiritual gene that multiplies throughout the body of Christ, totally unchecked.

No! I'm not saying there is a spiritually defective salvation through Jesus Christ. The precious blood of Jesus Christ will never lose its cleansing power. Anyone who calls upon the mighty name of Jesus with a sincere heart will find salvation. What I am addressing is something that happens after a person has accepted Christ as Savior.

In a previous chapter, I mentioned that birds of a feather flock together. People do the same as birds. The followers of Jesus separate themselves by levels of belief and obedience. People shift and flow like a river of flesh, seeking the level where they feel comfortable.

Therefore if any man be in Christ, he is a new creature: old things are passed away; behold, all things are become new. And all things are of God, who hath reconciled us to himself by Jesus Christ, and hath given to us the ministry of reconciliation. 2 Corinthians 5:17,18

Each flock, herd or denomination has its own flow. It's difficult to understand how such a wide variety of differences can occur in the same species of new creature in Christ Jesus, until you understand the story of the tuskless elephants.

Elephants become weak and tuskless from the inbreeding of that weak gene. In like manner, the Church becomes weak due to spiritual inbreeding. There are many defective genes flowing through the knowledge level of God's flock, of which compromise, fear and disobedience are but a few. As an example, it's far more comfortable to attend a church that doesn't believe in paying tithes.

Having a form of godliness, but denying the power thereof: from such turn away. 2 Timothy 3:5

When religion is the main course and tradition a side order, you have a form of godliness that denies God's power. It looks good, smells good and sounds good. Society accepts it because it does nothing, declares nothing and requires nothing. It's nonthreatening and socially acceptable.

People go where they feel comfortable and slip into a routine. That routine becomes a rut and few escape the trap. Herds of evangelical church attendees become uncomfortable when the gospel is preached, an altar call is given and they are asked to repent. They become offended in such a service.

You might say they can get as mad as an old wet hen because they're required to make a decision! The gospel of Jesus Christ is the truth and, therefore, confrontational. People don't like confrontation.

Some people flee confrontation to find a church that doesn't preach a born again experience or give altar calls. When they find one that's comfortable, it's weak and preaches a diluted message. They may sit with hundreds or thousands of people, but they have a social gospel. They feel safe and comfortable, surrounded by a large group of people who look, think and act as they do.

There can be doctrinal differences concerning water baptism, speaking in tongues, the length of the message or a myriad of other things. Unfortunately, this is where spiritual inbreeding causes spiritual birth defects.

And God said, Let the earth bring forth grass, the herb yielding seed, and the fruit tree yielding fruit after his kind, whose seed is in itself, upon the earth: and it was so. Genesis 1:11

Everything produces after its own kind! Many call themselves Christians, yet they don't know God and ultimately will die and spend eternity in hell. They never have repented and called upon Jesus to save them from their sins. They have attended church for many years but will find their place in hell, wailing in agony, because they are lost and don't know it. They gather in religious tradition and produce others exactly as themselves. They don't know the power of the risen Christ.

Not everyone that saith unto me, Lord, Lord, shall enter into the kingdom of heaven; but he that doeth the will of my Father which is in heaven. Many will say to me in that day, Lord, Lord, have we not prophesied in thy name? and in thy name have cast out devils? and in thy name done many wonderful works? And then will I profess unto them, I never knew you: depart from me, ye that work iniquity. Matthew 7:21-23

This is a tragedy to the men who never have told the truth of the gospel message to people who sit in darkness. However, we're not dealing with that group in this book. We're dealing with people who are born again. They're born again, but due to spiritual inbreeding, they became an exact duplication of the spiritually defective Christians who led them to Christ.

This group is usually weak in faith and commitment to the basic truths of the Word. The body corporate is comprised of Christians who, for one reason or another, are deprived of the sincere milk and strong meat of the Word on which to base their lives. The body becomes undernourished and weak when it lacks a properly balanced diet.

Their only examples of believers are those members of their own weakened and undernourished group. In turn, the flock begins to multiply by natural birth as young families have more children or by spiritual birth as others come to the Lord. With the lack of strong believers to set strong examples, these new-comers begin to take on the natural and spiritual attributes (actually defects) of the crippled Christians around them.

And I, brethren, could not speak unto you as unto spiritual, but as unto carnal, even as unto babes in Christ. I have fed you with milk, and not with meat: for hitherto ye were not able to bear it, neither yet now are ye able. For ye are yet carnal: for whereas there is among you envying, and strife, and divisions, are ye not carnal, and walk as men? 1 Corinthians 3:1-3

Having no other examples to disciple them, they grow in their spiritual walk. They think the mature Christians in their flock are examples of Jesus Christ in every way. Meanwhile, these allegedly mature believers actually are crippled Christians, deprived of strength, efficiency, wholeness or capability for service. This results in what I call spiritual inbreeding. Flocks of crippled Christians produce after their own kind. They duplicate themselves repeatedly, to become a group incapable of functioning as the Lord intended. There are multitudes milling around spiritually drought stricken waterholes, completely oblivious to the fact that they lack life-giving power that flows from the throne of God.

There are churches that get people saved, baptized, pray for the sick, expect miracles and reach out to a lost and dying world. These flocks receive a stronger message and are more committed to the truth of the Word, but we still see cripples in their midst.

And these are they which are sown on good ground; such as hear the word, and receive it, and bring forth fruit, some thirtyfold, some sixty, and some an hundred. Mark 4:20

In a strong flock, with the proper nourishment and the right examples, we find different levels of commitment. Their fruit production is 30, 60 or 100. There always will be different levels of growth and fruitfulness.

As healthy herds of elephants in southern Africa will include infants, youth, mature and aged, so is the healthy flock of God. The day the Lord returns to earth, it will be the same as it always has been, but there will be this requirement. We're required to grow into full maturity.

As newborn babes, desire the sincere milk of the word, that ye may grow thereby. 1 Peter 2:2

Just as the newborn elephant is susceptible to natural dangers and predators, so newborn babes in Christ are susceptible to spiritual dangers and predators. The newborn requires protection and guidance by the elders in the herd. The newborn in Christ Jesus requires care and protection. The mature ones guide them through their formative years.

If crippled leaders (who are the product of spiritual inbreeding) nurture these spiritual children, all they can do is produce another generation of "like kind." This vicious cycle continues, generation after generation, as crippled leaders teach a flawed, compromised message, which they think is the whole truth.

Multitudes of crippled Christians believe that God uses illness, tragedy and disaster to teach His people. It's nearly impossible to get people to accept the healing power of Jesus, once they have swallowed this unbiblical doctrine. I've seen people on their deathbed in absolute agony. They won't release the belief that God is receiving glory by teaching them something while He destroys their body.

In the animal kingdom, the strongest survive. The weak perish as predators stalk them in the wilderness. In the kingdom of God, the spiritually strong overcome and are victors. In the kingdom of God, the spiritually weak perish to the unseen spiritual predators who inhabit this dark world.

And from the days of John the Baptist until now the kingdom of heaven suffereth violence, and the violent take it by force. Matthew 11:12

The spiritually aggressive press into the things of God.

Are you satisfied with your spiritual life?

What is your outlook for your future?

Look at your leaders. Are they spiritually aggressive or are they crippled? You'll spend the rest of your life moving along with this flock. Are you prepared for that? Birds of a feather really do flock together!

Decisions that ultimately control the direction and destiny of your life are never easy. Governing your life and living by faith according to God's Word is not the easy way, but it is the only way. The decision is yours.

Chapter 11

WHO CULLS CRIPPLED CHRISTIANS?

In this dispensation filled with God's mercy and grace,
In Christ Jesus, we have found a strong hiding place,
Where our heavenly Father will never disdain nor disgrace,
As we live by His Word and look on His face.
— Rev. Ron Kussmaul, Johannesburg, South Africa

In chapter one, we took an intimate look at the lion, the great predator of Africa. We discovered that our particular lion was past his prime and was barely able to bring his prey down following an immense struggle. No longer the powerful killing machine over all his subjects, he was forced to prey upon the weak, crippled and stupid for his existence.

Our lion left the same scent upon the ground and still appeared to be the king of beasts, but his physical prowess was depleted. His only hope of living was to use the power of deception and fear. The antelope herds tremble in fear at the sight, sound or smell of the lion. He must perpetuate this illusion by deceiving his subjects into believing he's as strong and terrible as he always has been.

He knows the illusion won't always work, as his strength fails more each day. Soon, only the occasional stupid antelope will fall prey to him. Soon he'll look over his shoulder and the dreaded hyenas will be following him, working up the nerve to attack and finish him completely. His course is set and he can do nothing about it.

Humble yourselves therefore under the mighty hand of God, that he may exalt you in due time: Casting all your care upon him; for he careth for you. Be sober, be vigilant; because your adversary the devil, as a roaring lion, walketh about, seeking whom he may devour. 1 Peter 5:6-8

The Scriptures tell us our adversary walks as a roaring lion. He is not a roaring lion, but acts like one. A real roaring lion strikes fear in the hearts of all who hear him. The devil is attempting to do the same to you. The truth you need to discover here is that the devil is pretending. It's all a deception.

In 1993, I participated in the National Big Game Count in Zimbabwe. We finished our count at an isolated waterhole and returned to the banks of the Zambezi River for our last night. A storm front had blown through and the mosquitoes were not a problem, so we decided to sleep on cots under the trees.

At 1:30 AM, a lion roared. You can hear the roar of a lion in the zoo or on a recording. That roar is like the meow of a cat in comparison to being in the wild with the lion when he roars. *The roar* strikes terror in the heart. The sound may last a minute or longer. This lion roared every 45 minutes throughout the night. That made for a rather sleepless night, especially as we were without firearms.

While we were eating breakfast, the lion stood up and slowly walked away, in full sight of the camp. As we watched, we could see and feel the power within him as the muscles of his legs and back rippled with each step. He didn't have to deceive us into believing that he was king of the jungle (and our camp if he had chosen). We were convinced!

We never saw him all night. His roar was enough to get our attention and provoke a reaction. Your adversary, through deception (his roar), can get you to believe he has all power and control. When you become fearful, you give him that control and power.

Whom resist stedfast in the faith, knowing that the same afflictions are accomplished in your brethren that are in the world. 1 Peter 5:9

We're supposed to resist our adversary, not fear him. The word *resist* is *to oppose.* How does one resist or oppose the adversary steadfastly in the faith? Turn on your mind and begin to concentrate!

He that committeth sin is of the devil; for the devil sinneth from the beginning. For this purpose the Son of God was manifested, that he might destroy the works of the devil. 1 John 3:8

What are the works of the devil? Think about it. He steals, kills and destroys. He uses deception and lies to make you believe he has power, and causes you to accept the lie and become filled with fear. When you fall for the deception and accept the fear, you're in the hands of your adversary. You've put yourself there.

Now, back to our question. How does one resist or oppose the adversary? We resist steadfastly in the faith. The word *faith* in this context means *persuasion, conviction, assurance, belief and reliance upon Christ for salvation.*

We stand steadfast, knowing that God sent His Son to destroy the works of the devil. When Jesus uttered the words, "It is finished," His work was completed. We must believe the truth of the completed work of Christ on Calvary and the promises of the Word of God. When we believe in Christ, we don't believe or receive any deception of the adversary, no matter how much he roars and threatens.

It's as simple as that, and yet as hard as that. You must make the decision ruthlessly to accept the truth of God. This is faith. When you resist your adversary steadfastly in the faith, he will flee from you.

Submit yourselves therefore to God. Resist the devil, and he will flee from you. James 4:7

In Africa, if you happen upon a lion in the wild, you must not yield to fear and run. The instant you do, the lion is on you like a cat on a rat. You draw the lion to you like a magnet as he senses your fear. The first instinct of your fear is to run away. This will bring sudden destruction upon you.

The realm of the natural reflects the realm of the spirit. In the spirit, your adversary also can sense fear. When you manifest fear, you draw the supposed reality to yourself just as sure as the natural lion comes swiftly to the running man.

For the thing which I greatly feared is come upon me, and that which I was afraid of is come unto me. I was not in safety, neither had I rest, neither was I quiet, yet trouble came. Job 3:25,26

Is our adversary a roaring lion?

No. He moves about, attempting to convince you he is a roaring lion.

If he has so little power, why do so many Christians give such credibility to him by fighting him and praying deliverance?

1. Many Christians are convinced completely of the devil's existence and not nearly as convinced of God's existence, ability or willingness to help them.

2. They're weak in faith (trust in God) and well exercised in fear of the adversary.

How can they change this deficiency in trust?

There is only one method of breaking the cycle of fear and replacing it with a strong faith in God, but it takes initiative. The majority of Christians withdraw from the effort of developing a strong faith and trust in our heavenly Father.

So then faith cometh by hearing, and hearing by the word of God. Romans 10:17

People are lazy by nature and Christians are people, too!

Do you read enough of the Word through the week?

I don't have to answer that. You know the answer.

Chapter 12

A CRIPPLING DISEASE

Your faith is destroyed by this killer, unbelief.
From its paralyzing effects, there is seldom any relief.
It gives birth to a child of destruction called doubt.
Instead of God's blessings, comes the thief with a shout.
— Rev. Ron Kussmaul, Johannesburg, South Africa

How do crippled Christians develop this disease of the heart? Crippled Christians are a category of people that I call unbelieving believers. That may sound like a paradox to you, but that's exactly what they are.

These people hear the gospel message, cry out to Jesus, repent of their sins and find salvation. They become born again. They undergo spiritual regeneration. Their names are written in the Lamb's Book of Life. Unfortunately, this is the total extent of their ability to believe. They stumble through life as casualties in the kingdom, falling prey to their adversary at his leisure. They never realize there is anything beyond the salvation experience.

Think about the tragedies that befall Christians you know: constant sickness, divorce, adultery, drug addiction, premature death, financial disaster and all sorts of other things. You and I both know that the devil culls them (they become his easy target).

They become victims of the devil instead of victors in Christ Jesus–because of unbelief. People will not obey what they cannot believe, and disobedience to God's Word and commandments are the root cause of their destruction. They're not able to accept the promises of the Word of God at face value.

And being not weak in faith, he considered not his own body now dead, when he was about an hundred years old, neither yet the deadness of Sarah's womb: He staggered not at the promise of God through unbelief; but was strong in faith, giving glory to God: And being fully persuaded that, what he had promised, he was able also to perform. Romans 4:19-21

This passage from Romans tells us of Abraham's strong faith. He didn't consider the roaring of the adversary when he looked at the deadness of Sarah's womb and his own dead body. He "staggered not" at the promise of God through unbelief. We see many in the body of Christ whose lack of belief causes them to stagger at the promises of God. The unbelief causes them to stumble, as they fail to grasp the victorious life in Christ Jesus.

Do you remember that the great lion in chapter one was waiting for a special victim to cull? The old buffalo bull had dull hearing, poor eye sight and was stiff with arthritis. He no longer could run to escape as he staggered to the waterhole where his adversary, the lion of the African veld, was waiting for him. The old bull didn't have the mobility or speed to avert the inevitable disaster that stalked him. He found it difficult to get a proper footing for escape as he staggered to his feet and attempted to hobble away from the mud in which he was lying.

The crippled Christian is like that dull-of-hearing, poor-sighted, crippled buffalo. The old buffalo couldn't escape disaster while he staggered through the slippery mud that clung to him.

The crippled Christian attempts to escape sickness, marital strife, financial difficulty and other crises by staggering in the spirit. They try to make good their escape and avert the thing they greatly fear, as it comes upon them. They struggle to get a good footing because of the slippery sin in which they are lying. The sin of unbelief has resulted in the failure of many Christians.

Wherefore (as the Holy Ghost saith, To day if ye will hear his voice, Harden not your hearts, as in the provocation, in the day of temptation in the wilderness: When your fathers tempted me, proved me, and saw my works forty years. Wherefore I was grieved with that generation, and said, They do alway err in their heart; and they have not known my ways. So I sware in my wrath, They shall not enter into my rest.) Take heed, brethren, lest there be in any of you an evil heart of unbelief; in departing from the living God. Hebrews 3:7-12

They staggered at the promise of God with their unbelief. They were weak in faith and not fully persuaded that what God had promised He was able to perform. The Lord said they had an evil heart of unbelief. The Hebrew nation didn't enter into the Promised Land for one whole generation.

And being fully persuaded that, what he had promised, he was able also to perform. Romans 4:21

Few Christians are fully persuaded that God is able to perform what He said in His Word. The absence of total persuasion causes Christians to stagger at God's answer to problems. The answer is the Word of God. This plague of unbelief is widespread across the body of Christ.

Wherefore also it is contained in scripture, Behold, I lay in Zion a chief corner stone, elect, precious: and he that believeth on him shall not be confounded. Unto you therefore which believe he is precious: but unto them which be disobedient, the stone which the builders disallowed, the same is made the head of the corner. And a stone of stumbling and a rock of offence, even to them which stumble at the word, being disobedient: where-unto also they were appointed. 1Peter 2:6-8

The Christian who can believe on Him (Jesus) shall not be confounded, that is in shame or disgrace. Crippled Christians are unable to believe and, therefore, are in a constant state of being confounded. They stumble at the Word, being disobedient, as they find it impossible to believe. They cannot obey it in order to receive God's promises.

In this condition, they become easy prey for that old adversary, the devil and the demon hoards that follow him. Though he has no power over them, they succumb to his deception as they focus their attention upon the roar and let their fears run away with them. They create disaster in their minds. They exercise their fearful thoughts until they are overcome by imagined situations.

Fears live in the mind.

Fantasized **E**vents **A**ppearing **R**eal

They assist their adversary, yielding their power to him and draw the thing that they fear the most unto themselves.

While we look not at the things which are seen, but at the things which are not seen: for the things which are seen are temporal; but the things which are not seen are eternal. II Corinthians 4:18

One does not see or feel faith. Faith is a spiritual force, the ability to trust God and His promises courageously simply because He spoke them. If you have an area of your life in which you're not able to apply this kind of faith, that's the area where you believe God has lied! This may cut to the bone, but this is the core of the problem.

And we desire that every one of you do shew the same diligence to the full assurance of hope unto the end. That ye be not slothful, but followers of them who through faith and patience inherit the promises. For when God made promise to Abraham, because he could swear by no greater, he sware by himself Saying, Surely blessing I will bless thee, and multiplying I will multiply thee. And so, after he had patiently endured, he obtained the promise. For men verily swear by the greater: and an oath for confirmation is to them an end of all strife. Wherein God, willing more abundantly to shew unto the heirs of promise the immutability of his counsel, confirmed it by an oath: That by two immutable things, in which it was impossible for God to lie, we might have a strong consolation, who have fled for refuge to lay hold upon the hope set before us. Hebrews 6:11-18

Either God lied or He didn't! We have to make a decision on this self-induced plague called unbelief.

The majority of Christians don't bring the entire tithe into the storehouse, as Malachi 3:10 instructs. Is the Bible wrong about this? Did God make a mistake in this Scripture? If God made a mistake here, He could have lied about healing or salvation!

No. A thousand times, no! God didn't lie. Jesus didn't have a "bad-hair day" on the cross!

The majority of Christians don't tithe because they're not fully persuaded that it's their obligation. This weakness will cripple them. They keep God locked out. By their disobedience, they tie God's hands so that He can't intervene on their behalf in their finances. They have created their own weakness, as they stumble through unbelief and cannot receive the blessing of God's promise.

The areas in which you compromise or disobey are the areas in which you lock God out of your life and allow the devil to have full reign.

You now must fight your adversary, the devil, in your own strength. You've disobeyed the instructions of God, stumbled at the promise and willingly yielded your authority in Jesus Christ to the devil. If deliverance is to come, you'll have to overcome your adversary in the power and strength of your own ability (which is impossible) or you'll have to repent and cry out for mercy. It would be easier to obey God than to go through another self-inflicted detour on life's road.

Can you give me a reference in the Old or New Testament where unbelief or doubt is a virtue?

Not once in the entire Bible is a Scripture found that praises unbelief.

This makes me wonder why so many people live by such strong unbelief.

Chapter 13

THE ANTIDOTE

Faith is the spiritual force that cannot be seen.
But, through simple belief, it springs into being.
With many false teachings, ranting and raving they try,
Though Pharisees work hard, simple faith in Jesus will not die.
— Rev. Ron Kussmaul, Johannesburg, South Africa

Faith lives in a forest called "risk!" Without risk, there can be no real faith. If you know the outcome in advance, you don't have to trust God and exercise faith. How could you grow spiritually, overcome larger challenges and increase your capacity for greater results if you don't exercise your faith?

Have you ever wondered why there are so few risk-takers in the body of Christ? We're supposed to be one of the largest groups of believers in the world. It's simple. We have too few faith-filled examples to follow!

Faith in God is a subject that many scholars and theologians seem to hate with a passion. When you teach Christians in this area, it really "throws the cat among the pigeons," so to speak.

Repeatedly, I hear that you cannot live by faith. They say it doesn't work, but it's too late to convince me.

I've lived by faith in many countries of the world for over 34 years. I have a highly infectious, strong faith in Jesus. Doubt and unbelief bounce off me as a rubber ball. The thought that God might have lied about the wonderful truths of the Bible refuses to enter my mind.

Strong faith in Jesus is the ultimate and total relief,

For the devil's brand of fear and failure brought on by unbelief.

Yes, in the midst of these trials of self-induced hurt and grief,

One dose of faith in Jesus will prove the devil is still the thief.

Wherefore (as the Holy Ghost saith, To day if ye will hear his voice, Harden not your hearts, as in the provocation, in the day of temptation in the wilderness: When your fathers tempted me, proved me, and saw my works forty years. Wherefore I was grieved with that generation, and said, They do alway err in their heart; and they have not known my ways. So I sware in my wrath, They shall not enter into my rest.) Take heed, brethren, lest there be in any of you an evil heart of unbelief; in departing from the living God. Hebrews 3:7-12

God calls unbelief in the heart an **evil heart** of unbelief.

So we see that they could not enter in because of unbelief. Hebrews 3:19

The biblical record of God's people who failed to enter into His promises is a good object lesson.

Let us therefore fear, lest, a promise being left us of entering into his rest, any of you should seem to come short of it. For unto us was the gospel preached, as well as unto them: but the word preached did not profit them, not being mixed with faith in them that heard it. Hebrews 4:1,2

Please note. They failed to enter God's rest.

The first two verses of Hebrews, chapter 4, show a possibility of not entering into God's rest, even though it's a promise given to us through Jesus Christ. The Word preached to them didn't profit them because they didn't trust it.

For he spake in a certain place of the seventh day on this wise, And God did rest the seventh day from all his works. And in this place again, If they shall enter into my rest. Seeing therefore it remaineth that some must enter therein, and they to whom it was first preached entered not in because of unbelief. Hebrews 4:4-6

Unbelief was the thief that kept this group out of God's rest.

What does "God's rest" really mean? The word *rest* means *reposing down or abode; to settle down; to colonize.*

There's a dwelling place in God called "rest." That's where the people of God cease from their works. It's a place where all the struggles are over. Christians who have to struggle with the devil every day haven't found this place in God. They still are attempting to defeat the devil. We inherited the victory, not the fight.

There remaineth therefore a rest to the people of God. For he that is entered into his rest, he also hath ceased from his own works, as God did from his. Let us labour therefore to enter into that rest, lest any man fall after the same example of unbelief. Hebrews 4:9-11

There's both instruction and warning in this passage.

We're admonished to labor to enter into rest. This tells me that we'll have to work to reach this place in God. The word *labor* means *to use effort, to use speed and to be prompt or earnest.*

We're warned, lest any man fall after the same example of unbelief. The word *fall* means *to fall or fail.*

Not entering into the rest of God is to fall or to fail. Jesus suffered and died so we wouldn't miss the mark or fail to receive the promise.

If Jesus bled and died to provide a literal place of rest for me, I want it. In fact, I refuse to be denied. All I have to do is have faith, trust that the battle is over and rest in the victory Jesus bought on Calvary.

For whatsoever is born of God overcometh the world: and this is the victory that overcometh the world, even our faith. 1 John 5:4

It's the individual believer's faith in God and the ability to rest in the assurance of His promises that overcomes the world, not praying night and day against the devil.

That word *faith* means *persuasion, credence, assurance and belief.* It also means the *reliance upon Christ for salvation and constancy in such profession.*

Simple Bible faith in God is the antidote for the worst case of unbelief that ever existed.

Are you still fighting the devil on a regular basis?

Why?

He's defeated!

Chapter 14

DANGER AT THE WATERHOLE

As the shadows grow longer toward the end of day,
The place of quiet ambush at the waterhole is the lion's way.
The antelope, shoulder-to-shoulder, drink, so secure they stay.
Without remorse, the hidden lion thinks, they're just prey.
—Rev. Ron Kussmaul, Johannesburg, South Africa

The lions of the African veld know that the animals will throng to the waterhole to drink their fill. This daily routine has gone on for centuries and will continue until time ends. While the herd bunches up, it's easy to select a victim because the crippled and weak stand out from among their peers.

Why should it be any different with our adversary, the devil? Your church attendance becomes a pattern, a routine. The regular times of service have become the waterhole where Christians congregate, shoulder to shoulder. Mark 4 tells us the devil lies in ambush in and around churches.

The sower soweth the word. And these are they by the way side, where the word is sown; but Satan cometh immediately and taketh away the word that was sown in their hearts. Mark 4:14,15

If I want to find weak and crippled Christians to cull from God's flock, I'd go where they gather to feed and drink. The weak, crippled and stupid are easy to select, as they stand out vividly when they gather to get a sip of living water. Crippled Christians who have a guilty conscious because of hidden sin or compromise are easy prey for the unseen spiritual predators. Their spiritual garments, covered with spots and wrinkles, stand out next to those who live and walk in the light of the gospel.

Mark 4 says Satan comes immediately and takes away the Word that is sown in hearts. Most of the sowing of the Word takes place at church. What a great place for the devil to hang out and pick off weak, crippled and stupid sheep from God's flock. The church is the last place most of these sheep expect an ambush.

I received the infilling of the Holy Spirit on Monday, October 13, 1977, at 9:42 PM. I became a different person as the power of God infused my being. As the strong meat of the Word influenced my life, I grew rapidly in the things of God. I had no idea that God would call me out of the business world into full-time ministry and send me to South Africa with a mandate to "Quicken the body of Christ from the Equator to Table Mountain."

The church I attended grew rapidly. We were in the middle of building a new auditorium. One Sunday evening a guest speaker took up an offering for the building fund. Giving a seed of $1,000 toward the building project, I sat down thinking I was finished with my part of the offering. The offering reached $25,000 and then the flow stopped. The guest speaker had to "pull" for people to give.

I had a supernatural experience with God that I didn't expect. I was minding my own business, when the Lord spoke in a commanding voice, "Give your guns!" The command was so loud that I jumped to my feet in an instant. Every eye in the congregation turned to look at me. Deep within myself I said, "I don't want to give my guns. I don't want to do this." I burst into tears and announced, "God just told me to give my guns and I'm going to do it," and sat down.

My obedience to the voice of the Lord opened an avalanche of giving, and the offering grew quickly to $54,000. I missed that part because I experienced something that shocked me deeply.

As I sat down, the Lord opened my eyes, and I saw in the spirit. I saw a dark, shaggy shape standing in front of me, facing the front of the auditorium. It looked over its right shoulder at me with a confused expression, as if to say, "How did I get out here?" The sounds of the service were completely gone, and I was eye to eye with this thing. It walked down the row to my right until it came to the aisle, where it turned and looked back at me as if it wanted to return. I watched it walk up the aisle toward the back of the building and right through the wall into the night.

I turned back around in my seat and exclaimed within myself, "God, what was that?" The Lord answered immediately, "Oh, not much! You were just delivered from a spirit of idolatry."

Ye shall make you no idols nor graven image, neither rear you up a standing image, neither shall ye set up any image of stone in your land, to bow down unto it: for I am the Lord your God. Leviticus 26:1

I had a nice collection of guns that had become idols to me. I didn't know they were idols, but I had compromised that area of my life, and the spiritual predators had been watching. I felt clean that night as I drove home. Early the next morning I emptied the gun cabinet, took them to the church office and piled them on the pastor's desk.

I was born again, filled with the Holy Ghost and growing rapidly on the Word of God at the time of this incident. I had no idea I'd put my guns and hunting ahead of the Lord. What I found so astonishing was that when I made the decision to obey the instructions of the Lord and give the guns, the spiritual predator left and never returned.

This is just another tactic of the devil to tempt and trap unsuspecting Christians. You can create an idol in your life out of anything that you put ahead of your love for Jesus: guns, a car, a house, people, etc.

This happened in 1978 in Dallas, Texas. I gave away all my guns at the direction of God. In 1982, a deacon in a church came to me and told me the Lord had instructed him to give me a Smith and Wesson revolver. He wanted to know if he should put it in the offering plate or give it to me after the service. I received it after the service. I gave my guns in church, and they started coming back in church when the Lord could trust me with them.

Some of the deepest hurts and most bitter fights take place when families come together. They hold unforgiveness in their hearts for decades. Would it not seem that the same could happen with the spiritual family of God when they come together? I didn't say it was *supposed* to happen, just that it *could*.

Millions of Christians go to the waterhole (their church) with their guard down. They feel safe in a group, just as the antelope feel safe when they gather around their waterhole. "There's safety in numbers." At least that's what people say. People probably said that same thing during Noah's day. They scoffed at him because he was the only one in the world building an ark. The "safety in numbers" theory literally was all wet the day the flood came, but it was too late for the masses.

In the wilderness areas of southern Africa, one still needs protection from the dangers of wildlife. The incidents are rare, but every year wildlife and humans stumble into each other in awkward circumstances, resulting in death or serious injury. Accidentally getting between a cow elephant and her calf usually results in the death of the unsuspecting victim, while lions come into camp and drag people off in their sleeping bags. When a lion is around, it is comforting somehow to have the weight of a 458

Winchester magnum on my shoulder with a 510 grain bullet that produces over 5,000 foot pounds of energy. In certain situations, I like to be armed and dangerous–to be on the safe side.

If I'm going to a spiritual waterhole (local church) and there's the slightest chance of having to face a predator that acts like a roaring lion, I want to be armed and dangerous. The weapon of choice to use against spiritual predators is a sword (Bible). I carry this sword in two places, with me and in me.

For the word of God is quick, and powerful, and sharper than any two-edged sword piercing even to the dividing asunder of soul and spirit, and of the joints and marrow, and is a discerner of the thoughts and intents of the heart. Hebrews 4:18

I stand amazed at the number of weak, crippled and stupid Christians who arrive unprepared for a chance meeting with the adversary. They never carry a weapon (Bible) with them to the waterhole of their soul, nor do they have backup ammunition (Scriptures hidden inside their heart) for their own protection.

I believe the phrase is "sheep to the slaughter."

Chapter 15

THE GOOD NEWS

I'm safe at home in my comfort zone.
If anything happens I can always pick up the phone.
As long as I can hide away, inside I will have no fear,
Even though we all know, the devil is lurking near.
— Rev. Ron Kussmaul, Windsor, Ontario, Canada

There's a bully (the devil) living in your neighborhood (the earth) who likes to throw his weight around by stealing, killing and destroying. He can beat on you any time he wants. He can keep you intimidated, frustrated and in fear.

Fortunately for you, your Father (God) heard about it and got tired of it. He sent your older brother (Jesus) from a far place to beat the bully at his own game and destroy his works. The bully was defeated and his ability to push you around was shattered. Each time the bully sees you in the neighborhood, he trembles in fear because of what your older brother did. Just the mention of your older brother's name (Jesus) strikes terror in his heart.

Would that be a wonderful situation in which to live? You can!

And we know that all things work together for good to them that love God, to them who are called according to his purpose. For whom he did foreknow, he also did predestinate to be conformed to the image of his Son, that he might be the firstborn among many brethren. Romans 8:28,29

Jesus Christ, the Son of God, the King of kings and the Lord of lords gave His precious blood to forever settle the hold that sin had upon humanity. He rose from the grave as victor over all the forces of the adversary.

He was the firstborn among many brethren. Each of us has the choice to come by the way of the blood of the precious Lamb of God. I used this connection one Sunday in August 1964.

I was a young man of 22 and home after four years in the Air Force. I was attending the Nazarene Church, but I was fighting this "born again thing," and pride was holding me fast. When you've successfully navigated Vietnam and your whole life is ahead of you, you actually think you're going to live forever. All this was about to change on a wet Saturday morning in the deep hardwood forest and limestone bluffs of the Mississippi River Valley.

I entered the forest before dawn. I knew the game would start to move as soon as the rain stopped and the sun came out. I looked forward to some excellent hunting. I sat down and leaned back against a small white oak tree to wait for the rain to stop. I was in a crouching position against the tree when I noticed a 6 foot 10 inch Timber Rattlesnake coiled and sleeping two inches from my right foot.

When I sat against the tree trunk, I was 22 years old, and suddenly I felt like I was 72 years old. I looked into the face of death–only two inches away. This was the day I discovered that every person on the earth is only half a breath away from eternity–the one they don't breathe in.

I rose, backed up one step and shot the snake. It flew into the air, striking out at me and anything else within reach, its fangs dripping poison. Fear kept me riveted to the spot as we stared at each other. I felt the amazing presence of God enter the forest and I knew the outcome could have been completely different. Rays of sunlight filtered through the canopy of the forest. I looked toward heaven and, with hot tears running down my cheeks, told the Lord I would surrender my life to Him.

Pastor Attik gave the altar call the next morning by saying, "Sin is like a beautiful billboard along the roadway. It catches your attention. Though it looks beautiful, it is deadly. If we milk the venom of a deadly rattlesnake and hold it up to the sun, we see all the colors of the rainbow. It looks beautiful, but it's very deadly."

I thought to myself, "God, You told him what happened yesterday." I blinked back the tears from my eyes, hardened my heart and refused to surrender my life and keep my promise to God. I rarely attended the evening services, but that Sunday night unseen hands drew me to the meeting.

The pastor stepped behind the pulpit and looked across the congregation. He began to weep deeply for about three minutes. He looked up and said, "God has been on me all afternoon. Someone was supposed to accept Jesus as Lord this morning. I can't get any peace over this situation."

I leapt from my seat and ran down the aisle, slid head first into the altar and wept my way to Jesus. A glorious peace filled my life and the heavy burden of sin vanished in an instant. I was born again!

Jesus Christ became our older brother to defeat the devil (the bully) for us. He became the sacrifice, taking away the threat that hung over our heads because of the fall of man in the Garden of Eden.

He that committeth sin is of the devil; for the devil sinneth from the beginning. For this purpose the Son of God was manifested, that he might destroy the works of the devil. 1 John 3:8

Think of it this way. When Jesus Christ uttered the words, "It is finished," that's exactly what He meant. To ensure His followers got the message, He said:

And Jesus came and spake unto them saying, All power is given unto me in heaven and in earth. Matthew 28:18

Jesus Christ, our Savior and Lord, has all power! There's no power left over for the devil to use as the bully on the block. Please don't forget! The mention of the name Jesus strikes fear in this supposed bully. There's no power left for man-made religions except the power of mental persuasion. They have orientation, regimentation and ceremonies to hold their converts, but they don't give life everlasting.

Jesus Christ is the true Lion of the tribe of Judah. He paved the way for all who will come and bow before Him.

There was a man of the Pharisees, named Nicodemus, a ruler of the Jews: The same came to Jesus by night, and said unto him, Rabbi, we know that thou art a teacher come from God: for no man can do these miracles that thou doest, except God be with him. Jesus answered and said unto him, Verily, verily, I say unto thee, Except a man be born again, he cannot see the kingdom of God. Nicodemus saith unto him, How can a man be born when he is old? can he enter the second time into his mother's womb, and be born? Jesus answered, Verily, verily, I say unto thee, Except a man be born of water and of the Spirit, he cannot enter into the kingdom of God. That which is born of the flesh is flesh; and that which is born of the Spirit is spirit. John 3:1-6

Take the step of faith today and begin to live by faith in Jesus Christ, the risen Son of God. Accept Him as your Lord and step from darkness into the glorious light of His life and love. I challenge you to walk and live each day in the Spirit as a born again child of God.

But what saith it? The word is nigh thee, even in thy mouth, and in thy heart: that is, the word of faith, which we preach; That if thou shalt confess with thy mouth the Lord Jesus, and shalt believe in thine heart that God hath raised him from the dead, thou shalt be saved. For with the heart man believeth unto righteousness; and with the mouth confession is made unto salvation. Romans 10:8-10

Existing from day to day, living by the law of averages, holds little promise for your future. Oh, yes, just two other little things you should keep in mind.

1. Unseen predators are watching.

2. Jesus is Lord over all!

Call out and He'll hear your plea.

I was before man. Yes, I was before all.

I was before the sin that caused man's great fall.

You see, I was there and made the serpent crawl.

Now, with My blood you are saved when I hear your call.

Rev. Ron Kussmaul

New London, Connecticut

Chapter 16

THE BATTLEGROUND
OF THE MIND

When looking at battles you will find,
The toughest of all is the battleground of your mind.
The deception of the devil will mentally blind,
While the truth of God's Word will renew and free your mind.
— Rev. Ron Kussmaul, Johannesburg, South Africa

To receive Jesus as your personal Lord and Savior takes no special skill or wonderful talent. The door is open to all.

And as Moses lifted up the serpent in the wilderness, even so must the Son of man be lifted up: That whosoever believeth in him should not perish, but have eternal life. For God so loved the world, that he gave his only begotten Son, that whosoever believeth in him should not perish, but have everlasting life. For God sent not his Son into the world to condemn the world; but that the world through him might be saved. John 3:14-17

Anyone who wants–from the nicest person to the darkest of sinners–may come and be born again. Jesus Christ came for all. The only stipulation is that you must believe in Him. People from all walks of life come to the cleansing fountain and receive forgiveness for their sins and experience the power of the precious blood of Jesus Christ. Some surrender because of the power of preaching, but many others come because of tremendous stress, hopelessness or desperate situations.

Each person arrives at the foot of the cross on a different highway of life and in different spiritual, physical, mental, social and financial conditions. None are turned away and each leaves as a new creature in Christ Jesus.

Therefore if any man be in Christ he is a new creature: old things are passed away; behold, all things are become new. And all things are of God, who hath reconciled us to himself by Jesus Christ, and hath given to us the ministry of reconciliation; To wit, that God was in Christ, reconciling the world unto himself, not imputing their trespasses unto them; and hath committed unto us the word of reconciliation. Now then we are ambassadors for Christ, as though God did beseech you by us: we pray you in Christ's stead, be ye reconciled to God. For he hath made him to be sin for us, who knew no sin, that we might be made the righteousness of God in him. 2 Corinthians 5:17-21

The man, woman, boy or girl who is in Christ is a new creature. Old things are passed away and all things are new. When a person is born again, the *spirit* is renewed, but the *flesh* and *mind* are not. This is where the problems start.

I can't accept as fact that the lives of so many of God's people are in a continual turmoil because the devil is so powerful and works so hard against them. If we look through the Bible, we find God's people had major problems in their lives because of two things.

1. Incorrect decisions

2. Disobedience

But the word is very nigh unto thee, in thy mouth, and in thy heart, that thou mayest do it. See, I have set before thee this day life and good, and death and evil; In that I command thee this day to love the LORD thy God, to walk in his ways, and to keep his commandments and his statutes and his judgments, that thou mayest live and multiply: and the LORD thy God shall bless thee in the land whither thou goest to possess it. But if thine heart turn away, so that thou wilt not hear, but shalt be drawn away, and worship other gods, and serve them; I denounce unto you this day that ye shall surely perish, and that ye shall not prolong your days upon the land, whither thou passest over Jordan to go to possess it. Deuteronomy 30:14-18

Life and good, death and evil are set before His people. God tells them to keep His commandments, His statutes, His judgments and to walk in His ways.

I call heaven and earth to record this day against you, that I have set before you life and death, blessing and cursing: therefore choose life, that both thou and thy seed may live: That thou mayest love the LORD thy God, and that thou mayest obey his voice, and that thou mayest cleave unto him: for he is thy life, and the length of thy days: that thou mayest dwell in the land which the LORD sware unto thy fathers, to Abraham, to Isaac, and to Jacob, to give them. Deuteronomy 30:19-20

Life and death, blessing and cursing are before the people. The instruction is to choose life so that both they and their children may live. Many of the so-called *attacks of the devil* are the result of wrong decisions because of insufficient knowledge of the Word of God. The resultant disobedience from these decisions produces the exact opposite of the promises of God you expect.

1. Adam made an incorrect decision to eat from the forbidden tree. (Genesis 3)

2. Abram made an incorrect decision when he took Lot with him. (Genesis 12)

3. Joseph made an incorrect decision when he told his dream. (Genesis 37)

4. The Hebrew nation made an incorrect decision when they listened to the ten spies. (Numbers 13)

5. King David made an incorrect decision when he killed Bathsheba's husband and took her as his wife. (2 Samuel 11)

6. The prophet Elijah made an incorrect decision when he ran from Jezebel. (I Kings 19)

7. The nine lepers made a mistake in not returning to Jesus to give thanks. (Luke 17)

8. Saul of Tarsus made an incorrect decision when he captured and killed Christians. (Acts 9)

9. Ananias and Sapphira made an incorrect decision when they lied to the Holy Ghost. (Acts 5)

10. The devil made an incorrect decision when he tried to be like the Most High God. (Isaiah 14)

In the first nine references, each could have said, "The devil made me do it. The devil came against me. The fight was fierce." The religious order of the day would have agreed and been completely wrong. In each instance, the people made a decision and paid the price for disobedience. This includes David, the man after God's heart.

In reference number ten, the statement, "The devil made me do it," is correct. The devil did exactly the same thing as the people in the first nine examples. It was his choice. He made a bad decision and paid the consequences.

God made entry into His kingdom simple. Anyone can come to Jesus. You cannot pay your way in, nor can you be good enough in your own righteousness. All must submit and "believe" their way into the kingdom through the doorway of Jesus Christ. Praise God!

Many of you say, "I'm born again. What now?" I'm glad you asked.

You must do two simple, but not necessarily easy things. Live by faith and renew your mind.

Now the just shall live by faith: but if any man draw back, my soul shall have no pleasure in him. But we are not of them who draw back unto perdition; but of them that believe to the saving of the soul. Hebrews 10:38-39

The just *shall* live by faith. The Lord doesn't say it would be *nice* if a Christian could comply. He didn't give us an option, but stated *we shall* live by faith. A large section of the body of Christ falls into the category of unbelieving believers. They believe in Jesus, accept Him and find themselves in the body of Christ. This is where we separate the men from the boys as we grow up spiritually.

So then faith cometh by hearing, and hearing by the word of God. Romans 10:17

Too many of God's people attempt to live on His promises while their faith account is overdrawn. They operate with a faith deficit, unable to believe and receive the benefits revealed in God's Word. It doesn't take a theologian or a rocket scientist to know that if faith only comes to us by hearing, then we need to listen to more of God's Word than we do presently.

You no longer can live and think as you did before becoming a Christian. There must be change in your life, and it must start with the renewing of your mind. Let's look at a key Scripture that will put us on the right path toward victory.

My people are destroyed for lack of knowledge: because thou hast rejected knowledge, I will also reject thee, that thou shalt be no priest to me: seeing thou hast forgotten the law of thy God, I will also forget thy children. Hosea 4:6

The Lord said the lack of knowledge destroyed the people. They rejected His knowledge, and for that reason He rejected them.

They forgot or disregarded the law of God. As a result, He forgot their children or skipped a generation of their descendants.

The prophet didn't say they were destroyed for a lack of praying, but for a lack of knowledge. Too many of God's people live flawed lives in disobedience to the Word. They attempt to patch the faith deficit with the bandage of prayer. They use the name of Jesus and bind the devil, to no apparent avail. To live in disobedience to the Word of God is sin to the child of God. The name of Jesus loses a great deal of its might and ability when poured through a sinful vessel.

Precious Christian people tell me the strength of the devil's fight. They feel they need to pray for hours everyday over the protection of their family. They tell me all the different demons against which they do spiritual warfare until they're exhausted. When I look at their lives, I see a big mess and not a good Christian witness. I have to be honest with you when I ask, "What about all those hours of prayer and spiritual warfare?"

There's only one prayer that will bring deliverance to a disobedient person, and that's the prayer of repentance.

Sin is an unlatched door into darkness.

Chapter 17

IT'S THE THOUGHT THAT COUNTS

No matter how I struggle, fight and pray,
I always end up empty at the end of every day.
Though I try to believe, the blessings stay away.
Could it be my thoughts are causing this delay?
— Rev. Ron Kussmaul, Johannesburg, South Africa

et the wicked forsake his way, and the unrighteous man his
thoughts: and let him return unto the LORD, and he will have
mercy upon him; and to our God, for he will abundantly pardon.
For my thoughts are not your thoughts, neither are your ways my
ways, saith the LORD. For as the heavens are higher than the earth,
so are my ways higher than your ways, and my thoughts than your
thoughts. Isaiah 55:7-9

The wicked man is to forsake his ways, course of life or mode
of action. The unrighteous man is supposed to forsake his inten-
tions, plans, purposes and thoughts imagined. The unrighteous

man will have unrighteous thoughts, and when implemented as action, they cause him to walk in wicked ways. The Scripture tells us that there is pardon for this individual. If he turns to the Lord, he'll find mercy.

The Lord clearly points out that our thoughts and ways are lower than His thoughts and ways. If we could think God's higher thoughts, then we could apply them to our lives and walk in His higher ways. I find no Scripture in the Bible stating that we *cannot* think His thoughts and walk in His ways. The Bible is a book of God's thoughts. He put them there so you and I can read, listen, think and do His Word in daily life. It's a much higher way than we knew before we came into the kingdom, and it requires change in our lives.

Eat thou not the bread of him that hath an evil eye, neither desire thou his dainty meats: For as he thinketh in his heart, so is he: Eat and drink, saith he to thee; but his heart is not with thee. Proverbs 23:6-7

These verses deal with the type of people you should not have as friends. We want to look closely at the first half of verse seven, *"for* as *he* thinketh *in* his heart, *so is he."* What a person thinks in his or her heart dictates what he or she becomes. It's an awesome thought, but *the sum total of your life is what you think in your heart.*

Thousands of people are shocked when they first hear this, as it's human nature to blame others for the woes of life. They blame their parents, education, spouse, boss or the government. They blame everyone and everything, except themselves. It's easier to *place blame* than to *accept responsibility* for troubles, even though that's the first step to recovery.

As a man or woman thinks in the heart, so is he or she.

If you think the devil *actually is* a roaring lion that destroys whomever he wants, instead of walking in imitation of a roaring lion, you've empowered the devil to do things in your life, business and family.

As a man or woman thinks, so is he or she.

O generation of vipers, how can ye, being evil, speak good things? for out of the abundance of the heart the mouth speaketh. A good man out of the good treasure of the heart bringeth forth good things: and an evil man out of the evil treasure bringeth forth evil things. But I say unto you, That every idle word that men shall speak, they shall give account thereof in the day of judgment. For by thy words thou shalt be justified, and by thy words thou shalt be condemned. Matthew 12:34-37

These words of Jesus ring with the sound of finality. If Jesus said it, then it is true. The abundance that is in a person's heart is what he or she believes–whether positive or negative, good or bad, right or wrong. If you believe it in your heart, Jesus said you would say it.

Out of the abundance of the heart the mouth speaks.

And Jesus answering saith unto them, Have faith in God. For verily I say unto you, That whosoever shall say unto this mountain, Be thou removed, and be thou cast into the sea; and shall not doubt in his heart, but shall believe that those things which he saith shall come to pass; he shall have whatsoever he saith. Mark 11:22-23

These Scriptures have been the center of much controversy and strife. When I first found them in January 1978, I was ignorant to the fight in religious circles over the issue of biblical faith. I took the faith Scriptures at face value, as the truth. In my simplicity, I didn't presume Jesus would lie. I was looking for something that would work. When I applied the Scriptures the way they are stated, they turned my life around.

When the Lord said, "Whosoever shall say," He opened the door for the entire world to use this passage. It doesn't indicate Christians only. It states *whosoever.* Jesus said if the person does not doubt in his or her heart and can believe that the things they say will happen, they will have whatsoever they say.

This Scripture has two sharp edges, one that cuts in the positive direction and the other that cuts in the negative direction. Everyone believes *something*, whether good or bad, positive or negative. According to these verses, whatever you believe in your heart (and don't doubt) will happen if you wrap your tongue around it and say it.

You do have what you say if you don't doubt in your heart! We can say it this way. The life you have now is the result of the thoughts and beliefs you expressed in all your yesterdays.

We must deal with these verses, not fight and argue about them. They won't change or go away overnight or over the next hundred years, if the Lord tarries.

As he thinketh in his heart, so is he.

Option A. Imagine your life if you *think you have to defeat the forces of darkness by praying and doing spiritual warfare before you can have a successful day or protect your family*. As you think in your heart, so are you.

Option B. Imagine if you *think* Jesus defeated the devil for you. Your job is to live by faith and enter into God's rest, because the devil is defeated. As you think in your heart, so are you. This option appears to be one of God's higher thoughts that leads to His higher ways of life, as stated in Isaiah 55:9.

Unfortunately, these two options are *both* alive in the hearts of Christians. Both options are available to you, though the two are worlds apart.

Option A reveals a *big* devil and a *little* God. Something is wrong with this picture, but if you believe it, you can and do have it.

Option B reveals a *big* God and a *little* devil who is defeated!

The spiritual predators are watching to see which choice you make.

Out of the abundance of the heart, the mouth speaks.

Option C. Imagine if the abundance of your heart, say 55% or 65%, is negative and filled with fear and unbelief. In this scenario, you struggle to believe the promises in the Bible. The thoughts that are in *abundance* in your heart indicate what you really believe. We can say safely that negative, fear-filled unbelief taints 55% or 65% of your speaking. This is not a peaceful, restful situation.

Option D. Imagine if the abundance of your heart, say 55% or 65%, is positive and filled with faith and belief in God's promises. The thoughts that are *most abundant* in your heart indicate what you believe. We can say safely that positive, faith-filled belief energizes 55% or 65% of your speaking. This seems to be a better option to me.

Both options are available, though they move in opposite directions. Option C reveals 55 % or 65% of your words dictate fear, negativity and unbelief and make it difficult to produce blessings and live a successful life.

Option D reveals 55% or 65% of your words dictate a positive, faith-filled belief in the things of God. Let me say that merely 55 % or 65 % of the abundance of your heart would be little faith, but it is still faith.

Please check the abundance of your heart. Spiritual predators seek for any opportunity. You can and do have what you say if you don't doubt it in your heart.

Imagine that every word of the Bible is true and every word that Jesus said is true and will never change. We must live with these words. What if Jesus really meant what He said about "whosoever" getting what they say, if they don't doubt it in their hearts and believe that it will come to pass?

Option E. What if the abundance of fear-filled unbelief and natural-sense knowledge dictate the words you speak? They automatically cause things to happen, even though you may not want them to.

Option F. *What if the abundance of positive faith in your heart dictates your words?* The things you want would begin to come automatically. You are powerless to stop them.

These two options are available to you, though they produce two opposite results. With Option E, your words will produce results that are negative and filled with fear. It'll be hard to believe the promises of God. Frequently, you receive what you don't want and what you fear the most comes boldly into your life (as expressed by Job).

With Option F, your words will produce results in your life that are positive and faith filled. It'll be easy to believe the promises of God. You receive what you want, and what you believe from God's Word comes boldly into manifestation.

Please listen to yourself. Judge the words of your mouth. The spiritual predators listen intently to your every word. Can you even remember what you said earlier today or yesterday?

Could it be that Proverbs 23, verse 7, "As a man thinketh in his heart so is he," is incorrect or was interpreted incorrectly?

For as he thinketh in his heart so is he: Eat and drink, saith he to thee; but his heart is not with thee. Proverbs 23:7

Is it possible that God had a "stressed" day? Perhaps He really didn't mean what He said about the abundance of the heart causing the mouth to speak, or a good man bringing forth good treasure from his heart and an evil man bringing forth evil treasure from his heart.

O, generation of vipers, how can ye, being evil, speak good things? for out of the abundance of the heart the mouth speaketh. A good man out of the good treasure of the heart bringeth forth good things: and an evil man out of the evil treasure bringeth forth evil things. Matthew 12:34,35

Could it be that Jesus really didn't mean what He said about our words coming to pass if we didn't doubt them in our heart?

And Jesus answering saith unto them, Have faith in God. For verily I say unto you, That whosoever shall say unto this mountain, Be thou removed, and be thou cast into the sea; and shall not doubt in his heart, but shall believe that those things which he saith shall come to pass; he shall have whatsoever he saith. Mark 11:22-23

Though hard to comprehend, some of us really have difficulty believing that Jesus Christ, the Son of God, didn't tell the truth when He said, "whosoever."

Nature never argues with God. The fig tree discovered the power of faith words!

And on the morrow, when they were come from Bethany, he was hungry: And seeing a fig tree afar off having leaves, he came, if haply he might find any thing thereon: and when he came to it, he found nothing but leaves; for the time of figs was not yet. And Jesus answered and said unto it, No man eat fruit of thee hereafter for ever. And his disciples heard it. Mark 11:12-14

On His way to Jerusalem, Jesus found a fig tree with no fruit. He spoke to it and His disciples heard Him.

And when even was come, he went out of the city. And in the morning, as they passed by, they saw the fig tree dried up from the roots. And Peter calling to remembrance saith unto him, Master, behold, the fig tree which thou cursedst is withered away. And Jesus answering saith unto them, Have faith in God. For verily I say unto you, That whosoever shall say unto this mountain, Be thou removed; and be thou cast into the sea; and shall not doubt in his heart, but shall believe that those things which he saith shall come to pass; he shall have whatsoever he saith. Mark 11:19-23

I don't think God was short on filler text for Mark, chapter 11. Did He say, "Go ahead and blow the disciples' minds with that tree trick I showed you back in the garden"? I don't believe Jesus did it to show off His power. That doesn't coincide with His character as revealed elsewhere in the Word.

I have to believe this was an audiovisual display of the importance of our words–how we should think, speak, walk and live a victorious life.

Chapter 18

ESCAPING YOUR
THOUGHT BARRIER

God's promises are calling, so access I must find.
Somehow, I feel they're locked up in my mind.
Though I struggle with the devil, I loose and I bind.
I must be missing something; could it be I'm spiritually blind?
— Rev. Ron Kussmaul, Johannesburg, South Africa

The brain has a protective membrane that stops the penetration of many of the medications used by medical science to treat brain tumors. This protective barrier repels the attempt of these treatments to bring help to the afflicted area.

In like manner, the newly born again child of God becomes a new creature in Christ Jesus. He walks away from the life-changing experience with a renewed heart, but the same mind. The old sense-realm has an invisible barrier around the mind. Every new Christian carries this barrier into the kingdom of God.

This invisible barrier is the thought barrier. As the brain membrane forms a barrier that resists the penetration of medication, the old sense-realm thinking also resists penetration in the mental realm. This sense-realm thinking resists change brought by the revelation knowledge of the Word of God.

Most Christians never recognize that this old way of thinking has formed a mental barrier that separates them from receiving the promises of God. It's similar to the manner in which a prison wall keeps the convicted criminal separated from the general population. This thought barrier keeps us from entering into the center of God's will for our lives. Lack of knowledge captures us, and we can't enter into the flow of His divine favor.

I beseech you therefore, brethren, by the mercies of God, that ye present your bodies a living sacrifice, holy, acceptable unto God, which is your reasonable service. And be not conformed to this world: but be ye transformed by the renewing of your mind, that ye may prove what is that good, and acceptable, and perfect, will of God. Romans 12:1,2

The Word of God instructs us to present our bodies a living sacrifice, holy, acceptable unto God, and that is only our reasonable service to Him. The Scripture goes on to say: "Be not conformed to this world."

We must recognize that we are in this world but we're no longer of this world. The word *conformed* means *to fashion alike or to conform to the same pattern.* It's apparent the Lord doesn't want us thinking like the world.

One of the definitions of *conformed* in the *Webster's Dictionary* is *to act in accordance with prevailing standards or customs.* This is exactly what God does not want us to do.

I have given them thy word; and the world hath hated them, because they are not of the world, even as I am not of the world. I pray not that thou shouldest take them out of the world, but that thou shouldest keep them from the evil. They are not of the world, even as I am not of the world. Sanctify them through thy truth: thy word is truth. As thou hast sent me into the world, even so have I also sent them into the world. John 17:14-18

We're *in* this world, but we're not *of* this world. The two are, in fact, literally worlds apart.

"But be ye transformed by the renewing of your mind."

We're to be *transformed* which is *to change or transfigure as in the sense of metamorphose.* We do this by the *renovation* of our *minds*, which is the *intellect in thought.*

The word *transform* indicates that a radical change takes place. Notice it didn't tell us to be transformed by *adding more information* to our mind, but by the *renewing*, which is *renovation.*

Several years ago, I purchased property with the intention of growing the ministry office in the large guest cottage. I went to inspect the house after the previous owners moved away. My inspection revealed disturbing details I had missed when their furniture was in place. I knew not to say any words of disappointment or regret because my words have power.

The dining room appeared to be as long and narrow as a bowling alley and the plaster in other rooms was in bad condition. I searched the house for 45 minutes trying to deal with the situation that I found myself in. The more I looked from room to room I knew the problems were getting bigger the more I looked at them.

I was facing a major decision and I could do a quick cover up job and simply move into the house, but I would always know what was under the paint and drapes. The only solution was to do the work correctly!

To those who have ears to hear, let them hear!

I stood there trying to convince myself the simple cover up of paint, new carpets and drapes would accomplish what was needed, but eventually I knew it wouldn't work. These items would fill the need that was required to make the house a home. They represented the process of redecorating. When redecorating a home, you cover up the flaws and inadequate design features of the structure. You freshen up the appearance and hide the flaws that you know are there.

The Word of God isn't telling us to cover up the flaws of our old natural sense-realm thinking. When He says, "the renewing of your mind," He's telling us to change our minds by the process of renovation. The renovation of the house required a contractor and 12 workers. They worked for five weeks to completely renovate the house into what was really needed.

Step One was demolition. They destroyed two brick walls inside the house. They used sledgehammers to remove the plaster from the walls of seven rooms. I replaced ceilings and rerouted electrical wiring. When this was finished, I was ready for Step Two—the reconstruction.

This represents hard work and effort!

The Apostle Paul didn't tell the Romans to redecorate their minds by covering up the flaws of their old thinking. He told them they had to transform their thinking through the renovation of their minds.

The first step to the renovation of anything is to destroy the old and haul away the rubble. In the house, the workers broke down walls and removed layers of plaster. It took five dump trucks to haul away this rubble. Too many Christians have redecorated their minds by adding rooms with bits and pieces of spiritual information.

For I know that in me (that is, in my flesh) dwelleth no good thing: for to will is present with me; but how to perform that which is good I find not. For the good that I would, I do not: but the evil which I would not, that I do. Now if I do that I would not, it is no more I that do it, but sin that dwelleth in me. I find then a law, that, when I would do good, evil is present with me. For I delight in the law of God after the inward man: But I see another law in my members, warring against the law of my mind, and bringing me into captivity to the law of sin which is in my members. Romans 7:18-23

Paul said he experienced a continual warring within himself. This condition produces an up-and-down life that can start a cycle of backsliding and repentance.

For they that are after the flesh do mind the things of the flesh; but they that are after the Spirit the things of the Spirit. For to be carnally minded is death; but to be spiritually minded is life and peace. Because the carnal mind is enmity against God: for it is not subject to the law of God: neither indeed can be. So then they that are in the flesh cannot please God. Romans 8:5-8

The old natural mind (carnal mind) is death to the believer. Renewal in the spirit of your mind is life and peace. The carnal mind is at war against God. It will not submit to the law of God, and when this happens we can't please God. This paints an unhappy picture of a born again person who struggles to live in the promises of God. The old sense-realm thinking that isn't submitted to the law of God is at war with God's thoughts and ways.

A big problem I've discovered is that many Christians attempt to pray for mind renewal. It's impossible to create transformation this way. In the house, I could hear the sledgehammers pounding against the bricks and plaster to clear the way for the reconstruction. We brought in new bricks and new plaster to create a renovated structure. In the same manner, our natural thinking, established upon sense-realm knowledge, must fall under the pounding of the sledgehammer of hearing the Word of God.

It takes hard work and effort to remove the old brick and plaster of natural faith. People can't lay hands upon you and cast it out. You can't pray it out or cry it out. Only one thing will ignite the renewal of our minds.

So then faith cometh by hearing; and hearing by the word of God. Romans 10:17

We must replace our sense-realm faith with the God kind of faith that believes His thoughts and His ways. We do this by the repetition of hearing the Word of God.

The carnal mind that has not undergone the process of renovation holds on to the fear of the unknown, believing the devil can do to us whatever he wants. The carnal mind tells us to pray, fight and struggle to defeat the devil.

The renewed mind thinks all things are possible to those that believe. It lives day by day in the faith that Jesus destroyed the works of the devil and enforces his defeat. This person lives a victorious life in Christ Jesus and rests in the promises of God.

But if the Spirit of him that raised up Jesus from the dead dwell in you, he that raised up Christ from the dead shall also quicken your mortal bodies by his Spirit that dwelleth in you. Therefore, brethren, we are debtors, not to the flesh, to live after the flesh. For if ye live after the flesh, ye die: but if ye through the Spirit do mortify the deeds of the body ye shall live. For as many as are led by the Spirit of God, they are the sons of God. Romans 8:11-14

Does the Spirit of God lead you? If He does, the dictates of the flesh no longer control you. Your thoughts won't govern your decisions, nor open a doorway into the realm of the spirit for spiritual predators. Yes, they watch for an opportunity to steal, kill and destroy. As the lion of southern Africa patiently waits at the waterhole for his unsuspecting prey, so waits the destroyer of the souls of men.

And be renewed in the spirit of your mind; And that ye put on the new man, which after God is created in righteousness and true holiness. Wherefore putting away lying speak every man truth with his neighbor: for we are members one of another. Be ye angry and sin not: let not the sun go down upon your wrath: Neither give place to the devil. Ephesians 4:23-27

The book of Ephesians admonishes us to be renewed in the spirit of our mind. The word *renewed* is the word *renovated*. It tells us not to give place to the devil! The Scripture says that were not to give him a door of entrance in our lives. Living in disobedience to the Word of God and willful violation of His laws will open a door into your life and give a room where the devil can live!

The devil didn't attack you and take this place. You gave it to him through your disobedience. The devil is defeated and doesn't have the right to walk boldly into your life and push you around. If you disobey and open the door for the devil, he'll enter and occupy the space you've given him. Ask yourself these questions.

1. *Why fight a defeated foe?*

2. *Why give a defeated foe an open door to my life?*

3. *Am I a crippled Christian?*

4. *What do the spiritual predators see when they look at me?*

5. *Have I given place to the devil?*

You can escape the maze of incorrect doctrine and never-ending struggle with the devil through acceptance of faith in God. Childlike faith in His promises will set you free and keep you free. Develop the ability to accept God at His Word and never doubt His ability to fulfill what He's promised to do.

It's time for you to climb higher on the mountain of God.

CONCLUSION

I've confronted demonic activity in the lives of thousands of people throughout three continents and many islands. I've found spiritual predators tormenting people in Paris, London, Johannesburg, New York, Los Angeles and the list goes on. I've seen spiritual predators run wild in more than 30 different language groups in the vast areas of Africa.

Demons have threatened to kill me, verbally refused to come out of people, gone into convulsions and foamed at the mouth, as in Mark 9. They have made people crawl and writhe on the floor like snakes. One deaf and dumb spirit cut off the voice of a beautiful young girl and then communicated in sign language, though she didn't know sign language. Another person was in demonic bondage through her prayers to a Saint Christopher's medal.

The mighty name of Jesus set all these captives free–from the rich and sophisticated to the poorest of the uneducated in the isolated areas of Africa. It was not a problem to set them free from demonic power. The name of Jesus is above all names. Whether an educated sophisticate or uneducated, half-naked bushman foraging for food in the Kalahari Desert, their problems were the same. It's simple to understand if we see clearly.

1. Each sits in darkness without the knowledge of Jesus.

2. Each is a child of God in disobedience to the Word of God through lack of knowledge or sin.

I wish I could paint some gruesome picture, but this is all of it. If you don't know Jesus, you sit in darkness and spiritual predators have access to your life. You live by the law of averages. If you know Jesus as your Savior and don't live a Christ-like life, the spiritual predators have access to your life. You live life as a crippled Christian.

It's time for us to mature in Christ, know who we are in Him, and walk the life of faith by every Word of God.

Then was Jesus led up of the Spirit into the wilderness to be tempted of the devil. And when he had fasted forty days and forty nights, he was afterward an hungred. And when the tempter came to him, he said, If thou be the Son of God, command that these stones be made bread. But he answered and said, It is written, Man shall not live by bread alone, but by every word that proceedeth out of the mouth of God. Matthew 4:1-4

Remember, God is big and the devil is little!

WINGS Of BUSINESS

Preparing God's people to have dominion in the marketplace.

God instructed Ron and Mariette to teach His people success and financial principles. They began in Johannesburg on Thursday evenings. The revelation taught caused the crowds to grow and a Tuesday night meeting started in Pretoria.

Ron and Mariette travel the world continually, preaching in churches, teaching in conventions and conducting *Wings of Business Seminars* in various cities, usually as a Saturday or weekend event.

The men and women who attend the *Wings of Business* meetings testify to having new vision, energized hope, better understanding of God's Word on biblical success and amazing financial breakthroughs. The result is that many people have eliminated their debts, own their businesses or have multiplied their incomes.

For information about *Wings of Business* meetings, to schedule a seminar in your area or to invite Ron and Mariette to speak to your group or church, contact the office closest to you.

South Africa
+ (0)11-476-8392
Fax +(0)11-476-8757

USA
208-321-1274
Fax 208-321-1278

Canada
902-475-1955
Fax 902-477-0209

www.rkmi.org